If you've always wanted to start something bold — a business, an idea, a dream — but could never quite take the first step, this book shares with you how it can be done and what it really takes.

If you've ever asked yourself 'Is this really what I'm meant to be doing with my life?' then you might find inspiration in this story of everything I've risked and returned, lost and won, failed and fought for to ultimately find my purpose.

Derek .

derekhandley.org
twitter.com/dgh

Jan 2014
Sharya pora

Dear Greta,

The 'story' ... have a read :)

We are so proud of your stellar
rise and look forward to seeing
your journey unfold ...

With so much love and wishes
of bold choices, challenging times
& ever-ready inspiration.

Berde,

———

heart to start

The story of a global
start-up plus a guide
for turning your ideas
into action

to

start

DEREK HANDLEY

RANDOM HOUSE
NEW ZEALAND

A RANDOM HOUSE BOOK published by Random House New Zealand
18 Poland Road, Glenfield, Auckland, New Zealand
For more information about our titles go to www.randomhouse.co.nz
A catalogue record for this book is available from the National Library of New Zealand

Random House New Zealand is part of the Random House Group
New York   London   Sydney   Auckland   Delhi   Johannesburg

First published 2013
© 2013 Derek Handley

ISBN 978 1 77553 270 5
eISBN 978 1 77553 271 2

Design: Kelvin Soh and Minna Pesonen

Printed in New Zealand by Printlink

This publication is printed on paper pulp sourced from sustainably grown and
managed forests, using Elemental Chlorine Free (ECF) bleaching, and printed with
100% vegetable-based inks.

The quote on page 266 comes from *Pale Blue Dot: A Vision of the Human Future in
Space* (New York: Random House, 1994)

For Finn Emerson and Maya
as we discover each other, we uncover ourselves

CONTENTS

TURNING IDEAS INTO ACTION — THE FIELD GUIDE

II

PREFACE

Donation

I don't remember exactly when, but at some point I decided to give the year away. Kind of like how you give old clothes to the Salvation Army, or how you give money in those little envelopes you send off to a charity. In Brooklyn, New York, it's kind of like how you leave things on the stoop outside your home for people to pick up if they can make better use of them than you. *Just* like that, except I was giving one year of my life to causes and ideas that would move and inspire me enough to make a gift of my time and skills, to do whatever I could to help make something important happen.

Richard Branson and I were sitting on the couch together in the Temple House perched on the highest point of his home, Necker Island in the Caribbean. We each had a wine and I opened up about my idea of what I wanted to do next — for advice as much as anything. I shared that I'd tried a lot of things — some worked, some didn't — and eventually I'd ended up financially OK out of my series of entrepreneurial adventures. But it wasn't nearly enough. I wanted to start a totally new journey — worlds away from the one I knew.

'I don't want to just start another company. I don't want to start a business that doesn't, in some fundamental way, contribute to the greater good of humanity. I feel a new wave of thinking about to wash over us — that, as entrepreneurs, as dreamers and builders, we can do well for ourselves by doing good for the world. For me, the next year is a new chapter — it's a new journey to understand what this all looks like, to learn about what it all means before I get back out there and start again. So I've decided I want to give the year away. To be a student. To eliminate all possible barriers and excuses to seeing things with new eyes.'

I'd read and heard about people I loved and admired who lived in service of humanity their whole lives, and decided that, for just one year, I was willing to try it out. A donation of a year, a year of service, to people who were hatching plans at the intersection of doing good and doing well. We would work together to try to create something extraordinary. That was the idea at least. And for months now, it had been the plan — but I had never planned on giving all that time to just *one* person.

'You read my book, and I'll give you a year of my life.'

'Done.'

We knocked our glasses together. I'd just struck my biggest deal ever on a handshake with Richard, and I'd given it all away. No negotiating, no pushing, no horse-trading. No price, no special terms, no contract. Just one year, for one read. That was all I was asking for — the simplest pact I had ever made. As long as the problem was big enough, the cause was bold enough and I loved the idea enough — the year was his to work with. The token gesture I wanted in return was for him to read a book I'd just written to get his thoughts on the things I believed in. The things I learned through this story. The things I'd learned through living what's in this book. The things you're about to read.

I

01

Bankrupt?

I had just over a million dollars riding on a handful of shares, frothing at the brim with debt. Both the investments and I were resting on a knife-edge. My target: to make $100,000 for myself and a lot more for my partners. Why $100,000? Because it sounded round and even with a ring of freedom, and it was enough to start my own business to do things how I wanted to do them. I was 22.

Sweating it out in a small Melbourne apartment in October 2000, we were visiting my girlfriend Maya's cousins — and there I was, pretending to enjoy a holiday knowing that our financial future was hanging by a thread before we'd barely begun. As the share prices started slipping I knew something was up, I just didn't know what.

I could have sold the ones that I had risked the most on, Fletcher Challenge Forests, for more than 90 cents a share just a few weeks earlier while rumours were flying of a lucrative takeover of the company. I would have done well, repaid all my debts and student loans and been left with $60,000 or $70,000. For somebody who had just started his first job at an after-tax salary of about $20,000 a year, that should have seemed all right.

But no. $100,000 — that was the figure. At a buck a share I'd sell — and maybe I thought they were worth that. I had borrowed heavily, paying around 13 per cent interest, and every day that dragged on ate into my potential profits. I held on.

On 3 October the share price was not at its peak, but was still a respectable 80 cents. Just three days later it had tumbled to 72 cents, as people in the know seemed to think the takeover wouldn't happen. I still held on.

Then day after day, as the mystery of *when* the company was going to say something about its future became too much to bear for investors, the shares started to fall off a cliff. Without a lot of time to think, I started unloading chunks at 60 cents, 58 cents, 56 cents to hedge my losses to a break-even position until I was left with just over half my original holding. Hoping for a turnaround with the remainder, I still held on.

At this point I was still in control — if I'd quit right then I wouldn't have had a dollar to my name but that would have been the worst of it.

The next week we returned to Auckland. On 10 October the directors of the Fletcher Challenge Group announced the details for the breakup of the conglomerate and any hope went up in smoke. The energy division, in which I had the fewest shares, had the best outcome, being taken over by Shell for a huge premium over the price the shares last traded at; the building division was to be separated from the group and made independent because it was the strongest business; and after all the months of speculation of being taken over by one of the many parties swirling around like vultures, the directors stunned the market by confirming that *nobody* wanted to buy Fletcher Forests Limited. In what I thought was just a panic, the shares immediately plunged to 50 cents and the seven figures in my investment portfolio sharply turned into six. Still I held on.

The next two days were total carnage and by 12 October the

price was down to 43 cents — less than half of what it was just a few weeks before when I was flying high. I still hadn't made a decision to get cleanly out of everything, partly out of fear of what the devastation would look like in reality and partly in hope that it might turn back around. But by this point, I *had* to sell and get the hell out of this mess. I crouched on the lounge carpet, and calmly pieced everything together in my Excel spreadsheet to understand the size of the hole I was in. I knew there was a hole. I couldn't bear to look at it. I knew it was big. But how big?

All up, after everything was sold and all my loans had been paid off, the shortfall was about $100,000. Roughly five times my after-tax salary. Roughly the goal I'd tried to *make* just weeks before.

After a long morning alone, with my mind in turmoil and stomach churning, I decided to cut and run. I called Ray, my broker.

'What's my position if we get out of everything now except Energy?' I asked.

'Everything?' he questioned.

'Pretty much yes, everything.'

Confirming my own sums he said, 'Well, it'll definitely be about one hundred thousand that you'll need to cover, maybe a little more. So is this what we're doing?'

He went through each order line by line, getting my confirmation; I knew I didn't really have much choice. Hope, hedge and pray as a strategy had run its course.

'Yes.'

Ray sold everything except the energy shares and we cleared the shares into cash and paid off the debts I had racked up that enabled me to get that many shares in the first place. You see, using the equity that I'd put down in cash, I'd borrowed to the hilt to buy as many shares as I could so that my upside was as big as possible. Most of that million-dollar portfolio was built on debt — I didn't have a million dollars to play with, I'd leveraged to get it.

I'd lost some money. A lot of it was mine, but a good portion of it was other people's, my partners. My priority was to get them *their* remaining investment back and I needed to find roughly $100,000 to make that happen. I was wiped out, I had *nothing* left and at the end of the day I needed to find that money just to clear what I owed. Well, not quite by the end of the day, but within 72 hours.

One hundred thousand dollars. Twenty-two years old.
Borrow from Peter to pay Paul.
Where and who was Peter?
I hadn't figured that out yet.

If I could have described it to you then, I'd built a little leveraged hedge fund with a focus on conglomerate break-ups, targeting the arbitrage between the market's perception of the takeover premium versus the risk of the company's inability to maximise the value or sale of its assets. It was minimally diversified and leveraged to the hilt to maximise the upside. All that was true. It could have been written up in a memorandum to recruit investors, if my 'investment fund' had had a name, and if I'd *known* that was actually what I was doing. But I had no idea really — I was just focused on trying to make $100,000 so that I could start an interesting company and start living life my way.

For a few hours after making the call I sat in the apartment alone, a little frightened. It felt like ripping off a plaster that I'd been slowly peeling for a few days — but now I was worried about stemming the flow of red. Like a teacher phoning a parent to collect their naughty child, I called up Maya at work and spilled the blood.

'What is it?'

'You need to come home.'

Maya arrived to find me on the bed, sobbing. I cried like a baby and told her about the gravity of the situation. I was so scared for myself, and more so for my family, who were also tied up in this. It was all news to her, as I'd kept quiet on the overall position and just how far out on the edge I was hanging.

When I'd started this portfolio a few months earlier, I had set a more modest goal — several friends I'd dragged along into the scheme did as I'd advised, stuck to it and sold their shares as planned. Maya herself even borrowed $5000 from the bank, sold out when we said we would and made $2000 in a few months. Me, however — ever heard of 'Do as I say, not do as I do'? I got greedy. Or thought I knew better. Most likely both.

When we'd reached the target a few months earlier, we'd talked about selling out. By that point I'd made enough to clear my entire student loan and all other debts with plenty of cash to start a new adventure and be free from a salaried job for years. Maya had been emphatic that I cut it off there and sell, but I refused — pushing to stay the course a little longer — $100,000 had a nice even ring to it, and since things were going so well, why not let the dice roll just one more time and let them land where they land? In this case, in the deepest shit I'd ever been in.

Maya is often right in situations like this. She might not know the ins and outs or the whos and whats of an issue, but she has a sense about certain scenarios and timing. She stayed very calm. From where she was sitting, I suppose, nothing much would change: we didn't have anything anyway so how could it get worse? She was right, in a way. So there we were, two 22-year-olds with a couple of thousand dollars in the bank between us, who had to find $100,000 in 72 hours.

'Shall we call our parents and ask them to bail us out?'

'Never.'

Maybe we should have. But at the time, 'Never' was absolutely the right answer. We would navigate this alone.

Little did her mum and dad know that their daughter's boyfriend, a bright kid with a great future — supposedly — had already put the two of them in the hole for what most families would spend a decade saving for their first home deposit.

My first job out of university was less than eight months old and yet a few weeks earlier I had already resigned. (I'd done that when things were still riding high and it had always been part of my plan, even though the next steps weren't yet clear.) Now though, if I couldn't find a way to pull together a $100,000 tourniquet to strap the wound before I found a longer-term way to heal it, I was facing certain bankruptcy. And because I'd started out with no real plan, I had stupidly bought all the shares in my own name, not in the name of a company, so it would be *me*, Derek, who would personally go bankrupt. It was *my* name on the line. When you're looking at a loss that would take 10 years' average salary to recoup, if you know anything at all about making money then you know there's only two ways out: rob a bank or build a business.

'Suave, charming businessman orchestrates highly so-phisticated and untraceable gallery and bank heists, escaping by private jet with sacks of money while being chased by a gorgeous crime-scene investigator.' The quintessential Hollywood story: the original Steve McQueen version of *The Thomas Crown Affair*, one of my favourite films. Electric, glamorous, adventurous and tempting. However, I wasn't Thomas Crown, so I chose to start a business.

The financial collapse of my world inspired in me an acute urgency to *start* pursuing entrepreneurial financial wealth as opposed to salaried wealth. I always knew I wanted to do this and I was already preparing for it — but now my hand had been forced and it was the only possible answer.

Getting yourself into such a mess as a catalyst to building businesses to get out of it? To be honest I would not recommend it — but the few chess pieces left on the board cornered me in such a way that I really had no choice. There simply was no way I could pay off my own debts by climbing up somebody else's corporate ladder. Luckily, it was never a ladder I wanted to climb.

So as most graduates were happily toiling away at the first year on the job, in six months I had gone from making (on paper) more than triple my annual take-home salary, to getting into a hole of about five times that, and I somehow needed to claw my way out.

In what was to become a recurring theme of my life, I felt so old and so young at the same time, clutching to a roller coaster going both directions at once. I didn't feel on the same page as many of my friends — I had essentially bankrupted myself in a year (unknown to them) and was about to start a very different kind of journey. I didn't know a single person of *any* age (let alone mine) who was going to start a company. So to figure it all out, it was up to me and my magazines, my books and my brainstorms, my ideas and my intuition, my hard work, my heroes and my heart — and this thing called the internet.

In 2000 the world was still reeling from its infatuation with the internet's arrival. By then, people had realised they hadn't yet cracked the code of how to make businesses out of the 'dot com' era, but that didn't stop investors pouring hundreds of millions into young companies, then selling their shares to the general public just several months later at valuations in the hundreds of millions or even billions. A deal to merge the Time Warner media giant with the internet start-up AOL for US$350 billion marked the peak of the era of insanity. A few months later a confluence of events decided the jig was finally up — the champagne stopped flowing, the house of cards collapsed, the bigger-fool theory broke down, the music stopped and there were no chairs left in sight. Insert your own metaphor as long as it ends with 'the shit hit the fan'. The value of these internet stars plummeted overnight and helped trigger a deep recession; it was absolutely *the* worst time to get into the technology or internet industry.

So naturally, I was convinced the type of venture I should start was an internet-based technology company.

02

Shaped

Life isn't always about doing the right thing at the right time. It's as much about doing the wrong thing at the right time, and the right thing at the wrong time. I reckon it's important to seriously think about the opposite of whatever everybody else is saying and doing, or maybe just find a different take on it all. If people go left, I want to look right; if they condone, I'll consider whether to condemn; if they all agree, I'll want to know why. Now I'm not saying that you want to come across as a constant contrarian, but searching for what others aren't seeing sharpens the senses and questions the mind.

Did I start out this way? I don't know. We all start from *somewhere*, so it's probably useful to start there.

My mother grew up in the concrete jungles of Hong Kong when it was a British colony, and my father, out selling whisky from Scotland, said she was the most beautiful girl he'd ever seen. In 1978, I arrived. I don't know when one first begins to remember but I see a bungalow in the grassy undeveloped countryside of Fanling in the New Territories, an area bordering on China. I see the rusting watering can in the garden; the emerald green mosquito nets; kind elderly Chinese housekeepers and cooks I can dimly recall; a white Toyota hatchback station wagon emblazoned with the Pabst Blue Ribbon beer logo across the side. These, I think, are my first blurry memories.

We called my grandfather *Gung Gung* as that's what the Chinese call your mother's father. He was a trader. In 1946, he started a company, Empire Trading, and imported and exported things from all around the world into China and the region. Those two words exactly represented what Hong Kong was all about — empire and trading — and what it represented to the British Commonwealth as the final jewel in a crown that had been fading since the peaks of Queen Victoria's reign. Gung Gung started out importing and distributing plastic flowers, down the hallway from a spindly Li Ka Shing who was about 10 years younger and in the same game.

Dad was part of the establishment — he was a director at Dodwell & Co. in what was known as a 'hong', one of the few remaining great Hong Kong trading houses founded by a British, American or European merchant in the mid-1800s following colonialism around the world. Some of them survive today, such as Swire, Jardine's and Hutchison, now controlled by that very same Li Ka Shing, who went from selling plastic flowers down the hall to being one of the wealthiest men in the world.

At Dodwell's, Dad had a high-profile and influential job in charge of all the importing and sales of the vast portfolio of wines and spirits. With his position came privilege — the expat life that still carries on to this day in cities like Singapore, Shanghai and Hong Kong. He had an enormous apartment with spectacular Hong Kong harbour views, drivers and maids, secretaries, overseas holidays every year, the best schools for the kids, golf and country-club memberships — all paid for by the company. Sign up with Dodwell's and the entire lot came with it, along with

If you want to do something sharp and innovative, you have to know what went on before.

George Lois

the golden key — if you were senior enough — which unlocked unlimited use of the company's country bungalow in Fanling and the 15-metre junk that cruised the waters surrounding Hong Kong's 200 outlying islands. In a city like Hong Kong where it costs a fortune to survive, let alone live well, who in their right mind would give this up just as they were rising to the top in their late thirties?

Dad. In 1984 when I was six, he decided to abandon the trajectory he was on and start his own business. People say it takes a lot of courage to leave your job and start out on your own — perhaps it's like having a child, you never really know what it's like until you do it.

For us, overnight, our home shrunk to a third of the size; we moved miles away from the centre of the city where all the action was; my friends and my school were distant treks; the car, driver, clubs and holidays vanished; and along with them, that golden key.

We moved to what was then the outskirts — no expat children, no expat schools and no expats. The good news was that my grandparents had moved out there the year before to the exact same place, Pok Fu Lam Gardens. They lived in the apartment Block 2, and we shifted into Block 5, Apartment A on the twenty-eighth floor.

Shortly after this I started to understand what my parents did all day when they left home to go 'to work'. One year they held a Christmas cocktail party at their offices in Hollywood Road. There was drinking, canapés, laughing and hosting people I eventually learned were called 'clients'. This was the first exposure I'd had to business or what it meant to go out on your own. One of the lines of trade my dad was in was chocolate — specifically gambling chips and smokes — chocolate coins in gold wrappers bundled in little orange-netted sacks and chocolate sticks packaged to look like a packet of cigarettes. My first-ever paid task was to walk for hours on end from the western end of Hong Kong island through to the central district, armed with a few dollars, a notebook, a pen and a plastic bag, going door to door to every single store that might possibly sell this type of chocolate. The mission was to find and record the price, weight, number of gold coins per netted bag, how they were displayed and whatever else caught my eye, and to make good note of it all.

I came home from the heat and the 99 per cent humidity, and while I didn't get to eat the chocolates, I did get 50 Hong Kong dollars for my diligence, which I later learned was called competitor analysis. Fifty dollars bought three GI Joe action figures. Everything to me was measured in GI Joes — because they were a unit of value that was relatively fixed, and every single GI Joe was the same price no matter how many accessories they came with. The same price that is, until it changed; as well as being my unit of value, my GI Joes also taught me about inflation as the price rose from $10 to $20 over the years. I learned about foreign exchange through my parents' interest in the tail end of the nightly news where the newsreader lists the currency rates in that sing-song tone; Mum and Dad imported whisky, wine and oysters from the United Kingdom, so an exchange rate of HK$10 to £1 was good but HK$12 to £1 was bad. My very first memory of advertising was a commercial that my brother and I thought was really cool, until Dad asked what the ad was for and we couldn't tell him; we then learned the purpose of advertising and how shit an ad it must have been.

The boldness and upheaval of Dad's move taught us an early lesson to live by: that it was *perfectly OK to go backwards in order to move forwards,* and that if you're going to take risks you should time them well and probably take more while you're young. As children we witnessed first-hand that the ladder of life was not always straight up — and most importantly that it was just fine to let go of the trappings and status and not to let them define you. With Gung Gung on one side and Dad on the other, we had living examples of the responsibility to make your own way and create your own journey rather than buying into somebody else's. As these influences seeped into us in those early years, we probably never gave them a second thought. We are *all* a product of our surroundings, however, and we absorb what these people, places and possessions convey to us as what is normal, what is not; what is praised and what is panned; what is important and what is unnecessary.

Whether they intended to or not, my parents and my wider family immersed us in a city and an environment of games of chance and opportunity; people took risks every day to chase a dream or a fortune. The Chinese are superstitious and *love* to gamble. Whenever we went over to my mum's mother's house when the races were on, Pop (which is what we called our maternal grandmother after the Chinese name *Poh Poh*) would have the television on, showing horses wandering around the paddock, jockeys in all their different colours and patterns, some mounted, some walking alongside, and a pair of Chinese commentators pushing their favourite or slamming an unlikely chance.

Like clockwork, every 30 minutes, five minutes before each race, Pop would pick up the phone, call the Hong Kong Jockey Club and place her bets. There would be a moment's anticipation and she would walk over from the dining-room chair by the phone, sit comfortably on the couch and all would quieten. The attendants all rallied around the last stubborn horse and shoved him in and slammed the cage. The commentators silenced. The horses shuffled in their gates. *Ding ding ding!* a bell rang out, red lights flashed, the gates blew open, turf would fly everywhere and out came a dozen or more thoroughbreds rumbling down the straight with the commentator in full swing.

Pop wouldn't really follow the form or track record of the horses so much as the jockeys'. When a favourite jockey won, she would beam, and praise him like he was her own son; but when he didn't she would spew a stream of curses enough to make a gangster cringe, seamlessly switching between English and Cantonese. Of course we were never allowed to bet — we were far too young. But one Saturday she asked if I wanted to place one, just our secret. The minimum bet was about $10 of my pocket money — half a GI Joe. It seemed like a lot, but the odds were too tempting and it was like forbidden fruit. I bet, I won, and all of a sudden I had a new religion and a new reason to visit Pop.

Around the same time, my Uncle Junior took me on a trip to Lantau Island off Hong Kong with his girlfriend, Anna. I was about six. Mum gave me 50 Hong Kong dollars to last the entire weekend — a pretty good amount, enough for two GI Joes and a few sweets or Yakult drinks. We got on the ferry, a pack of playing cards came out and I was taught a basic form of poker, five-card draw. Before I knew it, the 50 dollars came out. Mum never said that gambling was a forbidden use of funds. Here we were, a six-year-old playing poker with a grown man on a swaying ferry. Two hours on the high seas. Head to head.

I'm sure I'd lost it all before we were even halfway there. I proceeded to cry as I not only didn't have any money, I had absolutely nothing to show for it and we weren't even at Lantau. Anna pressured him to give me my money back, but he refused. Who does this? Who gambles with a child and takes all their money?

Finally he relented, and agreed to give it back only if I promised never to gamble again.

I promised.

The money was handed back.

I stopped crying.

Twenty years later I was in Las Vegas seated at the World Series of Poker, so clearly his life lesson didn't work on me.

My first recollection of really thinking about what it takes for one human being to defy the odds and how the power of a single person can be so commonly underestimated was my dad's reaction to Richard Branson's television announcement of the launch of Virgin Atlantic Airways in June 1984. I'm sure his reaction was mirrored around the world by the smartest people in business and travel.

'He'll get crushed. No single individual succeeds in airlines, and the governments end up owning them.'

I was eight. Since then, almost no single individual *has* ever succeeded in airlines. Since 1984 dozens have gone under, been restructured or saved by nationalisation. Governments *always* end up owning them, either outright or through debt bailouts. For the most part, Dad was right; but so was Richard Branson, and Virgin Atlantic is still standing without a government bailout in sight, as are Virgin Australia and Virgin America.

Conversations about how people do these kinds of things and how ideas become a reality were commonplace in our home. In the living room around that same television there was a collection of technology like a fax machine and wireless telephone that became the topic of another night's lesson, this time in corporate and commercial law. My brothers and I wanted to know, *who* owns all these things? Geoffrey, my older brother by three years, was argumentative and forceful: we were adamant that Mum and Dad owned them of course, while Dad was adamant they didn't. Extreme confusion.

'Dad, I don't understand. We live in this apartment, we use this fax, that television and drink those wines and whiskies every day and nobody has ever come to take any of it. So why don't you own it?'

'They are owned by the company. The company that carries out all this business that Mum and I go to work to do each day. The company owns all these things, and we own none of it,' he tried.

'OK. So there's a company — it owns these things, we get that — but *you* own the company. So why can't we just say that you own these things?'

'Because I am not the company. The company is not me. It's not you. It's its own thing — it's its own person and I can tell it what to do but it's not me.'

'But at the end of the day, you own it, it owns the TV — so you own the TV. That *has* to make sense?'

'I do *not* own the TV. I own *nothing* except shares in the company. If people went around acting like they owned everything that the company owned, the world would be in a big mess. Companies often have different owners at the same time — yet how can three people own the television at the same time? They can't. The company owns the television, and as long as you are in charge of the company you get to decide how it's best used. So *everything* we use is owned by the company, and the company has decided we can use them for now. Get it?'

'No.'

Discussions like these would come and go and eventually

we either got it or we didn't. Although Dad tried his best, often we had to debate among ourselves and bring Mum in to try and make sense of it all. I have often wondered since why if at the ages of eight and eleven, us kids could understand this, 50- or 60-year-olds with decades of business experience continually forget the line between the corporate and the personal and make out like Bernie Madoff, running away with other people's money as if it were their own. Perhaps these guys never had a Toshiba fax machine in their living room as a child. Perhaps they never had a role model like my father.

Despite being surrounded by all this talk of trading and products and enterprise, *all* I ever wanted to be from around the age of five was a football player. I arrived at school early in the morning way before the bell in order to play football with anyone who was there. Every day after school, I played football until it was too dark to see the ball. I hunted down the best video tapes and books on how to be a great football player. Using them I devised my own training schedules and planned drills and practices that I would religiously follow alone or with others; for some reason I understood by then that if you wanted to be the best in the world at something you had to put in enormous effort, train hard and give it everything.

We played every single day on the concrete common areas surrounding the swimming pool in the centre of the Pok Fu Lam Gardens complex. There was a pair of off-white tiled flower boxes about the right width to act as a goal at each end of the rectangle recreation area. Anything that hit the tiles was a goal, anything above or wide was out; I with my average Cantonese and Geoffrey with his perfect street-smart slang would mix it up with the local Chinese kids of all shapes, sizes and ages. There was Bo Lo To who screeched quietly, about 13, the oldest and tallest so he always won the headers; Ghat Zat (Cantonese for cockroach), short, dark-skinned, scrappy and with a hoarse voice beyond his years — he came from the enormous Wah Fu public housing estate down the road; our trusty Pakistani friend Murad who lived in Block 4; and a whole host of others. On the concrete 'pitch' we had everything in common but nothing in common — for two or three hours every single day, we were bound together in the spirit of football. When there was enough of us for three or four teams of five or six aside, there was a sense of significance and adrenalin as the competition only then began to *mean* something — if you didn't win, you were booted off and had to watch on the park benches for several games until it was your turn again. I *never* wanted not to be playing — not for a moment — which meant *I never, ever wanted to lose.*

I was obsessed with the sport from the age of five, and up until I was about 11, I genuinely believed I could create a living out of it and had the total inner confidence that I would become a football star. This started to unravel after a series of realities hit me over the coming years and, as many of us are, I was forced to come to terms with fallen childhood dreams.

I had my first shot at starting a business when I was eight. My brother Geoffrey and cousin Dan in New Zealand had decided that they would get into the racket of buying faux-bronze signet rings from coin-operated bubblegum machines in Hong Kong, and selling them for a large profit in New Zealand. This was what came naturally to our family; my father and grandfather were both traders, so the grandchildren thought they would follow suit.

I had been left out so started my own line of business

with Dan's sister, Shareen, trading rubber watch protectors. We invested heavily: NZ$50 in an initial supply of 50 protectors that I packaged and shipped off to her in New Zealand.

The weeks and months floated by as the parcel slowly made its way to Auckland, by which time she'd forgotten all about them. I never really heard back from Shareen — she had, I'm sure, moved on to better things and while Geoffrey and Daniel's business was booming, ours was a bust. But it was a failure for good reasons. It's far too easy to start things on a whim and never really align the motivations and partners that will help you succeed. I had absolutely no interest in watch protectors and I didn't really care that much about making money either. To round it all off, Shareen also had zero interest in any of these things. The business fizzled and I went back to things I cared about: my GI Joes, football and by this time a new interest, space.

At the end of every year each kid at my school had to do a school 'project' — we could choose to write a report (more like a mini-thesis) about any topic in the world. I don't know why, but when I was nine I chose space, the planets and astronauts. I dove into exploring the universe and learned about every planet and space mission that I could fit in my nine-year-old mind. I drew diagrams and pictures of milky ways, space suits, spacecraft and on the cover I did a sketch of a fully suited-up astronaut. I became obsessed with space.

Around the age of 10 it seems everybody around the world has to switch schools but mostly they move along with the majority of the rest of their class; I eventually ended up in a place a lot closer to our new home but not a single childhood friend transferred to my new school with me. At South Island School I knew only one person — Murad, my footballing friend from Pok Fu Lam Block 4. In this new and uncertain environment, I think

I lost a lot of confidence. It didn't help that I was a very small child — *always* the shortest kid in the year group. At 12, in my Form 2 class photo I am so short that I am crowded out and you can only see a patch of hair.

Other than the usual things that start to evolve for teenagers like drinking, smoking and generally trying to be troublesome, the biggest thing to happen during high school was that when it came time to restart football in Form 3, I didn't make the cut. I wasn't training anywhere near as hard by this stage, I was getting distracted by new and interesting things and people and after some self-reflection I finally decided that this dream was over and I needed to search for new ones. A few unremarkable years passed and from an education perspective the only thing that stands out was history in Form 4 when I was 14. We were allowed to choose a topic for our final report — I chose John F. Kennedy.

Much like the focus on space and astronauts I'd chosen a few years earlier, I focused relentlessly on the Kennedys. They became an inspiration and theme in my life and remain so today. I was fascinated by JFK, a youthful figure with so much promise and vibrancy killed while still in his prime. The fact that the entire weight of the American government couldn't figure out how to solve the double crime of Kennedy's and Oswald's assassinations perpetrated right in front of their eyes further intrigued me, and as I discovered yet more Kennedys (Bobby, Ted and father Joe), the story became more and more captivating.

Because I was a new kid, was tiny and didn't know anybody, I became easy prey for the school bullies. It was never anything serious — just a bit of pushing, tripping and so on — but I really didn't know how to handle it. It does get you down when you're trying to settle into a new environment and have to face it every day.

I took my concerns home and one evening my brother Geoffrey was roped into the conversation because he never got bullied. In fact, he *did* the bullying so it was like getting expert advice. He gave me some pretty simple instructions that he swore would work — the next time you are bullied, tap the other kid on the shoulder, and when he turns around, punch him square in the face. Even if he's just tripping or teasing you and a punch is out of proportion, the instructions were clear: just step back, focus, tap and punch him in the face. Hard.

This, I thought, was an interesting technique — unorthodox and not exactly eye for an eye — but I understood the concept: reverse the tables and set a new expectation. Create a principle and a new normal that if you want to bully me, Derek Handley, no matter how big you are, I will punch you in the face. Hard.

Much like a lot of advice from people who've been there and done that, some ideas are much harder to do in practice. I went to school with my new plan. Ian the bully would be next to me in the line as we waited our turn to get on the court to play handball. He'd trip me up. Push me. Tease me. Just like always. And I'd be thinking *so* seriously about the idea of stepping back, aiming and punching him in the face.

But I never did.

Then one day up on the concrete football courts at lunchtime, I got into a tangle with one of the tallest kids in our year, Gerd. Blond hair, wiry, arms everywhere and a good half a foot taller than I was. I have no idea what the tangle was about but all of a sudden I was wrapped up with Gerd pushing behind me, and I thought, 'This is it, this is the real deal. No room to shoulder tap, but I need to punch him. *Hard.'*

I was half crouching as Gerd tried to get me into some kind of a hold with his gangly arms, using his back to push me down; I thought a moment and heard my brother whispering to me; I tried to understand in a split second what limb had the highest chance of pushing free; I focused everything I had on my right arm and entered into a flying, twisting uppercut using the entire force of my waist and legs to push my fist up through his hold, scraping past his neck, striking right under the jaw. His head flew back and my hand followed through, flying out in front of his face. Gerd stumbled back in agony, crumpled over onto the floor and I withdrew slowly, feeling like a steamroller had just crushed my fist.

The bullying stopped.

A couple of years later, I began to realise that my brother Geoffrey was a *tough guy*. He had a group of friends at school that dominated the Hong Kong social scene and nobody wanted to mess with them. They went by the lovely moniker *The Bastard Squad*. They loved to drink, do bad shit, skirt the law and get into scraps, and because many of them spoke Chinese and had tattoos of dragons and tigers, there were shady rumours they were associated with the Hong Kong gangsters, the Triads. True or not, just the idea that it *could* be was enough to put the fear of God into all the expatriate kids. I basically had my very own distant but benevolent 'Lord Protector' at one of those most difficult periods in life; when you're learning how to be a teenager and become a 'cool' kid, I was free to be myself and come out of my shell without ever worrying that I would be bullied again. Today I call this kind of arrangement 'air cover'; somebody who looks out for you so that you can have the confidence to chart your own course without fear of retribution or being laughed at should you do something stupid.

Geoffrey and I weren't close and the irony was that *he* bullied me at home constantly from when I was about four until I was about 14. But word quickly got around that if anybody *else* tried to bully me anywhere, at any time, for whatever reason, they would be dealing with the closest thing we had to a local school mafia.

I wasn't to enjoy my new security for long, however. Two years earlier, on 4 June 1989 I had witnessed a day that remains etched in the memories of Chinese and Hong Kong citizens around the world. On that day, the Chinese government drove tanks and marched soldiers into Tiananmen Square, Beijing, to break up a sit-in by university students pushing for a dialogue on democracy. I sat on the carpet, glued to the television, watching the stories and images dribble out to the world. This was a pre-internet era under a tightly controlled communist regime and news didn't come quickly, but the theme was clear: hundreds of students peacefully protesting were being killed by soldiers who were trained to protect them.

One man became an icon by standing up to a row of tanks. The power of that image: the solitary, faceless individual in a simple white shirt and black pants, casually holding a plastic shopping bag as if he was on his way home, having completed a domestic chore before stepping in front of a column of vehicles of war. He swung his bag and skipped from side to side as the tank wiggled its way forward to get around him. He climbed on top, and knocked on the turret like you'd knock on a neighbour's door, in an effort to turn these guys around. Nobody knows what happened to him.

In less than a decade, the government that had sent in those tanks would be back in control of Hong Kong after 155 years of British Rule. From that point on and into the early nineties any family in Hong Kong who had the means sought to flee. Hong Kong Chinese people poured into Vancouver, Sydney, Auckland, London and San Francisco — anywhere they could get a passport and guarantee their children a good education. My mother's sister Zarina had moved to New Zealand when she was very young. We had visited her regularly since I was two and my younger brother Calum was born there, so we had a long-standing connection. Emigrating increasingly became a topic of conversation around the dinner table.

For every generation there are a handful of people who do extraordinary things that define a moment or a sentiment. Each of us choose the ones that sear themselves into our character, or perhaps the icons choose us and bury themselves deep into our subconscious: back then, it was the unreasonable courage of 'Tank Man' standing up for what is right in the face of something very wrong. What became known as the Tiananmen Square massacres paved the way for another major fork in the road. Two years later, we made plans to get out of China's way, and head to New Zealand instead.

03

Experiments

One of the first times I started to think independently and make up my own mind about how I wanted to do things was when I was 15, in maths class. It's not that I hadn't made my own choices earlier — I had — it's just that some scenes are far crisper than others when I play back the reel of youth in my mind, and this was one of them.

In September 1992 we landed in Auckland to start a new chapter. I arrived to a world of expansive green spaces, clean air and blue skies that had almost no resemblance to the concrete, skyscrapers and excess that I'd just left. Selwyn College was nothing if not liberal; you were largely left to your own devices and those who succeeded either formed a strong bond with certain teachers or had enough motivation to chart their own course. I found maths relatively manageable and because it is a very black and white subject — you're either right or wrong — I decided I wanted to pursue total mastery of it as a personal experiment and get 100 per cent. I didn't particularly love it and nobody expected me to do particularly well in it either, having never before shown glimpses of mathematical genius. But love was not what this was about — there was no real aim other than a personal experiment to perfect the perfectable. This was the first of many such personal experiments. For one year, I didn't really care about any subject other than maths.

I remember the teacher vividly for two reasons. Firstly, he was a relatively elderly man, tall, slim with the side of his right hand permanently covered in chalk from using his hand as his blackboard eraser. The second thing I remember was that I couldn't find the value he was adding, or the passion in his work. About a third of the way through the first term, I decided this was a poor use of my time, and asked to speak with him after class.

'Sir, I think I'm going to use these times to study in the library and do the material alone, if you don't mind.'

'What?'

'Well, I find it difficult to concentrate in here and I think it might be best if I focus in the library. If I struggle with anything I'll come to you for help.'

'What? I'm afraid you can't. That's not how it works. During these classes you need to be in *this* classroom.'

'I understand. But if we think about the goal, which is to get a good grade at the end of the year, I think that this method is not the best way *for me* to do that. So, I've talked with my parents and they are OK with me just studying in the library.'

I didn't understand the objections — to me, it was the only logical and sensible option. I was definitely not trying to be difficult or special. I simply felt I knew a better way for *me* and I had to have the confidence and faith to back it. I felt it was the right choice and my parents had no problem supporting and trusting me.

The teacher was visibly distressed and dubious about my chances, dismissing the nerve of the lout with the long black hair and even blacker Metallica T-shirt. He told me quietly that I was destined to fail and was writing my own 'F'.

Unfazed, I walked out of the classroom and spent every

single maths time slot in the library as promised; I created a plan of action and mapped out all the various possible answers, and studied hard at home as well. The next (and final) time I walked into that classroom was for the exam. Many weeks later, when the grades arrived in the mail in a tiny manila envelope the size of a postcard, I ripped it open and immediately saw 'Mathematics: 98 per cent'.

I was shattered. The experiment I had set up was an experiment of me against me — and I had failed.

I'm far from a maths genius and that's not what this is about — I would later suffer heavily in the face of calculus at university. What it *is* about, however, is that I learned that when you set a goal, and create a plan on how to get there, and put a lot of energy and focus behind it, you can make things happen, even if other people don't believe you can. It also showed me just how important it is to have support — in this case from my parents — when you make bold decisions. Most importantly, it showed me that when you believe something is right for you even though it is not the normal or accepted route — in fact, *especially* if it is not the normal or accepted route — if it makes sense to you, then *you* have to have the sense to make it happen.

In a new country with not much to do and no freedom to get around (too young to drive and public transport barely existed in Auckland at the time), I began to spend a bit more time on computer games like the Nintendo and Sega Mega Drive but couldn't believe the prices Kiwi kids were being charged for the pleasure of a little Mario Bros. Frustrated, I was driven by justice as much as profit to rectify this situation; the worst thing was that the kids across the country probably had *no idea* how the system was screwing them. I devised a solution to screw the system right back and sent a small order to my friend Ken Kwok in Hong Kong requesting him to ship me consoles and a few dozen games I knew would sell in New Zealand. I then took ads out in the free classified newspaper, the *Trade & Exchange*, as well as on Teletext, a kind of pre-internet version of the internet that you accessed via your TV. Like many entrepreneurial opportunities, this situation arose from a combination of gaps in information, networks and action that existed in the market; this enabled me to sell what Ken sent me for a huge mark-up but far cheaper than local prices.

Intellectual property and digital rights management were something that children in Asia were brought up to ignore. Starting with the Apple II in the early 1980s, computer games and programs were simply pirated; you went to a store, pointed at what you wanted and they burned it on a 5-inch floppy disk. A few years later, the same thing happened to the Nintendo system; clever people created a method that converted all Nintendo games on expensive special plastic cartridges to a universal 3.5-inch floppy disk format that could be copied. We went to the local mall, pointed at the miniature pictures of the Zelda and Double Dragon games from the thousands on offer, the man behind the counter burned a few disks, we handed over 20 bucks and everybody was happy. The only respectful way to buy a game. But not so in Auckland; all you could buy were the official games, and even they were twice the price of their equivalents in Hong Kong.

My dad gave me a few marketing tips to experiment with. I created console and game bundles that made it easy for the buyer to set themselves up in one hit. The trick with these bundles was to throw in the games that were harder to sell and cheaper to buy, along with the headline acts of the big sellers, forcing people to take the good with the bad yet charging the same per game price regardless.

I became a regular fixture in *Trade & Exchange* and our home became a trading hub for dodgy second-hand computer games. With every new console, the game-makers would try to outsmart the pirates. The Sony PlayStation was no different; Sony put out new disk readers that needed a special black CD underside for the PlayStation to read it. However, all the pirates in Asia are a hell of a lot faster and smarter than one Sony Corporation sitting in Japan. Within weeks they created a simple gold spring mechanism that, when put into the top of the machine, quietly enabled you to run *any* CD that was a copy of a legitimate game. In Hong Kong I had only ever known this way of playing games — years later you would see this unfold in music with the advent of Napster and now it unfolds in every sector that makes the transition to digital — from books to games and soon, on a mass scale, movies. It plays out in any sector where the wisdom of the crowd might possibly be more valuable and attractive than the wisdom of a conglomerate.

Today, something has to be *so* much better in a variety of ways to rise above this death spiral. The quality of access, purchase experience or the good or service itself has to have an impact or people have to feel empathy in order to hand over money for digital experiences rather than just going out and stealing them.

With a string of small successes behind me, my confidence was growing and with the games I started making enough money to start thinking about what I wanted to do with it. I furnished my room with a big television and entertainment system, bought some guitars and even planned a trip to Japan with my best friend. Then I ran out of ideas.

At 16, I started to think about how the world worked — how people created things, how companies made things happen, how people got jobs — why some people got rich and others didn't. That year I'd read a book on how a group of New Zealand bankers figured out how to buy a collection of the country's major assets from the government and sold them off at huge gains to the Kiwi public in sharemarket listings. As much as I was shocked that this could even happen, I just wanted to check out what this sharemarket thing was all about.

I started to get very interested in shares and would read about the companies in the newspaper every day. I was interested in how they communicated, what they purported to do and how they made money. I decided I would take $5000 of my gaming savings and pick a company — I pored through the several hundred options and decided to put my chips on a business that I understood and could relate to. The Warehouse — founded by an inspirational figure, Sir Stephen Tindall — is the New Zealand equivalent of Walmart. It pioneered importing goods from all around the world to bring greater accessibility to ordinary New Zealanders at unbeatable prices. I loved the similarities with my gaming gig. After checking the prices daily on Teletext, I decided to dive in.

I soon encountered a problem: being 16 I found that I couldn't legally enter into contracts to buy or sell shares. But that was just another challenge and there had to be a solution waiting to be found. It's in times like these that I rely on mental vignettes of my grandmother, Pop. I was about six, we'd left her apartment just after she'd lit up a cigarette and walked straight into an elevator where there were clear 'No Smoking' signs plastered on the walls. The cigarette remained lit. Another passenger entered the lift on the next floor, saw her shrouded in a cloud of smoke, pointed at the sign and protested at her disregard for the laws of the lift. Unfazed, she responded coolly, 'I'm not smoking, I'm only holding.' The doors opened and we walked out.

For every 'No Smoking', there's an 'I'm only holding' waiting to be found. I hunted around, flicking through the Yellow Pages, and called up broker after broker requesting their account opening forms to be mailed to our home. When the forms arrived I squinted through the screeds of fine print looking for anything that would catch me out. Almost all of them had somewhere on the form that you had to sign and say that you were 18. But one didn't: Direct Broking. It was clear through their information pack that you had to be 18 to buy and sell shares, but they hadn't designed their forms to ensure that you signed confirmation that was actually the case. I have to be 18 to buy or sell shares — got it — but I don't have to be 18 to open an account? So I filled out the form, sent it back and three days later, a shiny plastic card arrived in the mail:

Derek Handley
C4X41X1

The account number through which millions of dollars of shares were bought and sold by the time I left university; and the account number I still hold today. I was never again asked if I was 18. I just picked up the telephone, called in my orders, paid up when my shares were due to be paid for, and banked my cheques when they arrived.

So with my newly minted account number, I phoned in my order and bought my first lot of shares in The Warehouse. I started checking the Teletext daily after school, continually reloading the page (the mid-nineties version of clicking 'Refresh' in your inbox or on Facebook) in the hope that something interesting would happen. Most days when I refreshed nothing much would; maybe the shares would go up or down by a few cents. Refresh. Nothing. Refresh. Nothing.

Then one day, something happened. I was busy refreshing Teletext in between whatever it was I was watching on TV and noticed that every time the page refreshed, the price of the shares went up. Refresh. Up. Refresh. Up. Refresh. Up.

I couldn't believe it. I'm sure I looked over my shoulder to check if somebody was messing with the Teletext. I was sitting on the couch, drinking Coke and watching music TV *while* I was making hundreds of dollars? How could these two things possibly be occurring at the same time? But sure enough, they were.

It turns out that The Warehouse was on a streak; the company was making big profits, all the analysts said it was a 'buy' and people just kept buying. Within a few weeks I'd made thousands of dollars from sitting on the couch. No phone calls. No games. No bundling. No advertising. Just me, the couch and my Warehouse shares going through the roof. I thought to myself, 'This is the way forward.'

Where would I be if I hadn't found a broker whose forms hadn't forced me to accept the supposed limitations of my age? This underscored to me that you have to *act* to make things happen and push for an angle in every situation. When somebody says no, find creative ways through. Break a rule? Fix it later. But whatever you do, *start*, and then look for the gap that you can break through to get to the other side.

From the age of 16 to today's 34, I have never once in my life met anyone that works at Direct Broking, but that's been perfectly fine by me. By the time I'd left school I'd expanded my portfolio of shares to all manner of companies, from tomato growers to timber manufacturers. I had read most annual reports, announcements and the ins and outs of the takeovers, sales or breakups of every company on the stock exchange to learn how they worked, what they did, how they made money and what they did to be good corporate citizens — I didn't understand all of it, but it did teach me a lot about things I had known nothing about.

As my gaming business got busier, the home landline phone kept ringing and people kept turning up at the door to pick up their games. My dad demanded an end to it.

'This has to stop. The phone can't keep ringing. You have to shut your business down — this is a home, not an office.'

I thought this was totally bizarre coming from a guy who had spent his whole life in a business that was so interconnected with our home. Why wasn't he passionate about helping me build this into a real entity?

I hunted around for a means to carry on my trade and the answer came quickly in the form of a mobile phone shaped like a small brick. It cost a fortune but enabled me to carry out my business wherever I was: in my room, at lunch during school, at the park. Wherever. I was on call. My friends started calling me Del Boy after the less than savoury and perpetually unsuccessful market trader Derek 'Del Boy' Trotter from the long-running BBC sitcom *Only Fools and Horses*. Whatever — it was 1995 and I had a mobile phone.

After several successful years of consistent trading, I met my demise through two intersecting paths. The first was an internal thing — a dwindling in passion. I became less and less interested in gaming, my heart wasn't really in it and everything started to suffer. Secondly, I got spooked by what I thought was my first brush with the law (although in hindsight it was just standard big-boy scare tactics). Getting more and more confident that I was serving a tidy niche in the second-hand gaming market, I started to get bolder and invest more in advertising. What started off subtly ended up with blazing ads — white on black to stand out on the page — headlined:

'PlayStation Games. Damn Cheap.'

A few days later, a mysterious man who didn't know much about games called me up and asked a few questions. A few days after that there was a curled-up scroll from Sony Corporation's legal department awaiting me in the fax machine.

The prices I offered were so low that Sony knew the games either had to be fake, imported or stolen. They sent their tirade, threatening in the way that only lawyers can threaten — it was your standard 'cease and desist' letter. I never told my parents and I was just about to leave for university so I thought perhaps I'd close this chapter and focus on the next one. In hindsight, I don't imagine there was a lot they could have done to me, but they genuinely had me shitting my pants and since by this time Sony PlayStation was the only gaming system in town, I thought that perhaps the timing was good to pack up shop and find a new adventure.

When it came time to decide what to do for university, I chose architecture. I love drawing; I love the design process of solving a problem visually, and imagining things that might exist in the future. As much as my side activities in business were fun, I had no great passion for it — not then; design and architecture however had started to really inspire me. I decided with my parents that I would move 800 kilometres south of Auckland to New Zealand's capital city, Wellington, and attend the Victoria University School of Architecture and Design. Part of the reason for going was that I wanted to see what it would be like to be independent and out on my own; part of it was that Victoria University seemed to be the best place in New Zealand to immerse myself in the world of architecture.

What I didn't expect was that the students in design and architecture would study and work on their drawings and models 16 hours a day. It wasn't just the young first-year students trying to make an impression; I saw the final-year students *five* years ahead of us basically *living* in the studio.

I decided very quickly that I would never be one of these people, even though it may have meant lower grades. I thought this approach to university was all wrong — I couldn't see how this sort of carry-on was going to make me a better person. Did I want to be one of those people in five years chained to my drawing table or in the model room? No.

I was very, very lucky. My mum never went to university and my father was the first of his family to have done so; whatever else they did for us in life, I get the feeling that making sure we had a chance to get an education was paramount. My parents paid my tuition fees and my living expenses, which I remember at the time were about $4000 a year for classes, and about $8000 a year for accommodation and living costs (New Zealand is not a particularly expensive place to go for a world-class education). I am grateful that I never had to worry about how it was paid for, and I focused on the search for new thrills and new experiments.

I landed in Wellington just before my eighteenth birthday. On 24 February 1996, Mum gave me a card, that has followed me everywhere, either pinned to the inside of my notebooks or up on my wall where I can see it. On the cover was a quote from German philosopher Johann Wolfgang von Goethe.

I don't know if she chose this particular card because of exactly what it said or because in my final year of high school I had won the Goethe prize for German, but it resonated strongly with me and underscored a fearlessness to take risks and dream dreams.

Whatever you do, or dream you can, begin it. Boldness has genius and power and magic in it.

Goethe

I think you have to look for things that give you freedom, freedom to learn, to make mistakes and try things. My parents gave me that freedom by paying the base of my way to university. I saw it as what university was meant to be about — freedom and learning on your own as much within the system as outside it. To me, the idea that you went to university to *study* 110 per cent of the time was for the birds. You went to university to learn how to live, just as you go to work to live your life, not live to work.

At every turn I tried to take a different angle to increase the time I had to do the things I wanted to do and make enough money to have the maximum amount of fun. My first year at university was 1996. In the dorm there was no web access and I had to share a phone with 50 students, so I installed a phone line, a fax and internet connection in my room and paid for it by renting it out by the hour. When the people voted in as presidents of the student residences couldn't get their act together to organise the annual end-of-term party, my neighbour Lee Prebble and I organised it ourselves in a few days, charged everybody $20 and made enough beer money from it for a whole year. Everybody in design and architecture was constantly taking and developing photos for their projects and I thought the cost of developing them was far too high. I set up a self-serve system in the library where you filled out a form and dropped off your roll of film in a box — I was useless at making things so I got my friend Mark to construct it and opened for business. The box did the hard work collecting the film, and each day I picked up a bag and shipped it off to a national processor, clipping the ticket in exchange for the hour I spent in the library each day, giving students their photographs and taking their money.

But as many successes as there were, there were a good number of disasters. I tried to launch a city guide in Wellington and spent hours pounding the streets trying to sell the idea to restaurants and bars. Depressingly I only ever had one taker when I needed 50 to make it work. I spent months working on a plan to create a noodle bar in the city as I became obsessed with ramen and thought Wellington should be too. In my second year I imported 2000 Tamagotchis — the hottest kids' toy in a generation — digital, egg-shaped pets that needed to be fed, cared for and nurtured virtually by pushing buttons in response to their alarm and chirps. My brother Geoffrey was in charge of sourcing them to hit the market while they were hot but by the time they'd landed (two months too late) the fad was over, they were banned from schools and I only managed to sell about 50. That left the other 1950 to chirp away in a storage cupboard in my flat.

Throughout the years, I borrowed my entire student loan, and invested it in travel, entrepreneurial experiments and shares. I saw it as freedom and an interest-free debt that I would never be forced to pay back if I couldn't afford to. I saw it as credit that would always be at the very end of the line for repayment, therefore I should take the freedom it afforded for experimentation. I knew that never again in my life would I be offered a no-strings-attached loan to take to the limit. I had absolutely no fear of debt, aware that I had an entire lifetime ahead of me to repay it should something go wrong. This was my private budget to see what I could do *outside* of the system, so that by the time I graduated I would have as much experience of as wide a range of things as possible. And if they all failed and I lost everything, I simply couldn't see how that was a bad thing — everybody was starting from ground zero once they graduated anyway, right? I figured the risk of starting at step minus one on a ladder that went from zero to a hundred was only marginally different from starting at zero. Plus, I was sure I'd acquire a kaleidoscopic set of battle scars and war stories before I'd even hit the real world.

In my final two years at university I conducted two major experiments. I decided I would use some of the money I had made to invest in a trip around the world to see what was happening out there. The only trouble was there just wasn't enough time in a school year to sneak in a six-week globe trot when each semester was 12 weeks long and I wanted to be back home in Auckland for the summer break to be with my family.

By now my belief in the time value of university was at an all-time low. I thought there were just too many weeks and months allotted to learn subjects and pass exams, and that actually degraded the ability to learn — if students were forced under pressure of compressed durations they would learn better and pass faster. At the same time I became interested in perfecting the science of sleeping and had learned that many great men in history, men like Churchill, Edison and Kennedy, had mastered the art of the nap.

At the beginning of the final term in my third year at university I established a plan to get my sleep down to four hours a night, and free up another four hours in the day. With my extra four hours each day I'd complete all the coursework in the first six weeks, I'd schedule my trip to start halfway through term, and arrive back the day before exams commenced. I promised myself that I'd take some books on the trip and on the planes, trains and automobiles I'd study whatever I needed to know to pass.

My lecturers all agreed to go along with my experiment; I did some basic research on sleep patterns and it ended up being a lot easier than I thought it would be, based on two simple decisions. First, I kicked off sleeping seven hours a night, and then gradually woke up 15 minutes earlier every day until I'd shaved off the full four hours after two weeks; next, I included one 30-minute nap each day around mid-afternoon and learned how to get myself to sleep within minutes.

I was really tired to begin with but then it just became normal. The bonus was discovering that working alone in silence through the earliest hours of the morning became a zone of efficiency and creativity. I spun around the world for weeks visiting friends and great cities before returning for exams.

My final year's experiment was a fascination with the sports-betting market. I used all my funds to create ideas for complex sports-betting algorithms in an attempt to devise models to statistically beat the odds set by the bookmakers. I then made the bets to back them. While this was mildly successful, what I really discovered was that the bookmakers took a ridiculously large margin, which made no sense in the age of digital technology. Just as online share trading had removed the margin sharebrokers charged for manually buying and selling shares, I saw this as an eventuality for the bookmaking industry too. A seed that was planted in my mind and remained there for a few years to come.

By that same year I had already switched majors to study both finance and architectural building studies, but had chosen not to fully qualify as an architect. I was very ready to get out of there. In what would turn out to be a prescient decision, this change required that I take a more environmental and sustainability-focused approach to my architecture studies; at Victoria University the faculty were world leaders in the art and science of making buildings fit into their natural environments, minimising their energy needs through better architecture and renewing their power supply through natural and renewable energy sources.

What I concluded at architecture school — seeing all the graduates from earlier years who had returned to teach us — was that this was not the life I imagined as an architect. I also noticed that my favourite architect in the world, Tadao Ando, was not even a trained architect. Something was very wrong with this picture.

If I was to design and build my own vision, my own buildings, I needed to be the client, not the architect. The client was a business, a businessperson or a person of wealth. I needed to be *that* guy and once I was that guy, if I wanted to, I was sure I could then be an architect of whatever building I wanted.

As much as I loved the idea of architecting ideas, the idea of being subservient to somebody else's ideas became less and less appealing by the day. I would learn about this type of conflict much later but in essence it is the confusion of drivers and passions that often leads people down the wrong path in life. What made me want to go to architecture school were factors that I wrongly interpreted as meaning I wanted to actually *be* an architect — I enjoyed using pencils and pens. I liked drawing buildings and how they looked on paper in 2D. I didn't care as much for the three-dimensional spaces they produced and the functions they needed to perform. I liked the stark contrast between the expressive, conceptual freedom of an *idea* and the detailed, specific accuracy required in portraying it so it could be brought to life. I liked the idea of things like drawing and being creative more than anything; I was drawn to the idea of having a *vision* and sketching it out until it had a chance of becoming a reality.

The misinterpretation of drivers can be life-threatening — not because it threatens your health, at least not directly, but because it threatens how you spend your life. People — parents, teachers, the world — can be too simplistic when they make assumptions about a young person based on what they see on the surface.

What you love doing is not necessarily *why* you love doing it. Just because you are a great chef doesn't mean you will have the skills, tenacity, people, marketing and financial abilities to imagine, start, build and run a restaurant. Just because you like creativity doesn't mean you should choose advertising or the arts as your profession. Just because you like maths doesn't mean you should be a mathematician.

Whatever we are naturally good at during our education should never automatically be assumed to be what we should educate ourselves in for life. People often find much later on that the joy they found in the things they loved when they were younger has been killed by making it too much like 'work', or dissipated by ignoring it altogether in favour of 'career' as they get older.

How we should approach it is to consider not only the *focus* of the work — the type of work, the subject, the activity itself — but just as importantly, the underlying *drivers* that motivate us. Those motives can be applied much more broadly than just the obvious: a love of cooking could reveal a love of hosting or the accuracy of a formula turning out just as it's imagined. A love of maths could be masking a love of analysis, the collecting of data, or problem-solving that could be applied in many situations where maths is nowhere to be found. The surface nature of the work can trick us into not understanding the deeper reasons we enjoy it.

What I ultimately concluded was that for me, it wasn't about the drawing or structures at all — it had nothing to do with the buildings. What it was, was the idea of picturing inspirational and beautiful things that don't exist today but *could* exist tomorrow, and creating the detailed plans to make them happen. It wasn't about the architecture of buildings then, and it isn't about the architecture of buildings now — what it took me some time to understand is that it's only ever been about the architecture of a *vision*, and chasing that vision until it becomes reality.

04

Maps

I was all about doing the different thing, and cutting my own cloth when university wrapped up, but I lemming'd out and tried to get a normal job. Why? I'm not sure. I guess I hadn't quite thought of anything else to do, but I also think I'd had enough of fringe ideas, at least for now. I wanted to experience being a small cog in a big machine; I wanted to stand around the water cooler and hang the swipe access card from my neck; I wanted to have performance reviews, get a 3 per cent raise and get ridiculously drunk at the annual Christmas party. I wanted to see what it was like on the inside in the outside world.

With only a vague idea of what I thought I might want to be when I grew up, I applied to recruitment programme after recruitment programme as the last days of term quickly ticked over. I thought I'd work in maybe business or finance, as I'd studied those subjects (as well as architecture of course, but I already knew I didn't want to do that). Twenty or more applications, and no replies.

I exaggerate. I got two short phone calls — a brief conversation with Macquarie Bank in Sydney, and another with the Bank of New Zealand, where I'd applied to be a currency trader. I'd heard a lot about the trading lifestyle, 'Ferraris at 30 and burned out by 40'. I thought I could do with the Ferrari at

30, and was sure I was smart enough to escape before I burned out. Since I'd messed around in shares I thought maybe this was for me, but something about the idea felt like wading through oil: doing nothing but moving digits, making nothing but money, employing nothing but capital and contributing nothing but liquidity to the future of the world. Either way, it didn't matter — no second interviews from either bank and no first interviews from anybody else. I resigned myself to the situation, packed my few things and returned home to Auckland for summer, where I poked around here and there, hunting for any final graduate recruitment programmes still accepting latecomers.

The Fletcher Challenge Group had such a programme. The group of companies was New Zealand's teetering testament to the 1980s conglomerate, modelled on the Japanese ideal of taking over the world one industry at a time. Building, oil, construction, gas, forests, pulp, paper. It was as old world as you could get, all fading maroon marble floors and mahogany-panelled walls, but at this point being open was more important than being inspiring, so I applied.

I wrote to them about dreams of conglomerates and played to the notes I thought they might want to hear. A few days later I got a call asking me to show up at a middle-market motel in a park for a full day of assessments. I was far more intrigued by the idea of a day of experiments than any job at the end of the line. So far I'd been the one conducting experiments — this was the first time other people were going to be conducting them on me. I showed up ready to battle and along with 49 other kids was put through the ringer for eight hours on presentations, prioritisation, group behaviour, leadership assessments, inbox management tests, maths tests, verbal tests, personality tests and tests on tests. It was like something out of a movie, orchestrated by an attractive pair of women who weren't much older than us. There followed second interviews and third interviews, group interviews and solo interviews — I can't be certain but I'm sure there were even interviews on interviews.

Somehow, after having never even got to the interview stage for every other major corporate in the country, I'd hustled my way past 500 applicants to 50 and experimented my way down to the final 10. In the tiny grey office overlooking the driveway of our home, I picked up the phone one afternoon to be told, 'You've got a job.' Marketing Assistant with Fletcher Challenge Forests, starting pay $28,000, start date 22 February 2000.

Forests?

Forests.

Plant a seed, grow a tree, wait 30 years, cut it down, saw it up and ship it out. Imagine working in an organisation where the product takes 30 years to create!

On my first day, and most likely within my very first hour, a grey-haired grizzly older man came close, and like an unkind wizard he stooped down to me with these words, 'Welcome to the first day of the rest of your life.'

I'll never know why they put me in Forests, to be honest. There was no serious marketing function and I was the only marketing staff so I was hazy about what exactly I would be assisting, but who I was assisting was clear enough — the first and only person who has ever technically hired me, my boss Geoff Bramley. Gentle, softly spoken, a good man as a first boss. I did exactly what he said — for a while — and that would get me to about lunchtime so I began to experiment in the afternoon to make things more interesting. I patched the 'New Kid' stripes on my shoulder and went around walking and talking to everybody in every department and began to collect a portfolio of activities that I had nothing to do with and no place being involved in. After a while, Geoff started to trust me a little and became a supporter of the walking and talking and a co-conspirator of building this portfolio of activities.

My role grew and grew, expanding to developing a web strategy one day, and then analysing and presenting customer satisfaction insights to management the next week; then helping organise the staff socials, reviewing in-store point-of-sales material and building an 'intranet' (an internal 'internet' for companies, which in the late nineties were all the rage). I even did a market analysis on a specific type of wood for Japan and eventually I collected the mother of all things that had absolutely nothing to do with anything I was qualified to do: trekking back and forth from Auckland in the tiny company charter plane each week to find out why a mill was shipping wonky wood to the Japanese, who liked it straight.

Kawerau isn't a place you'd want to move to. It's poor, tough, and there are no jobs. But it became home to one of the most fascinating things I'd ever done. I was there to do a brown-paper exercise which seemed simple enough to me: start at one end of things, map every single step of how things appear to be *today* and finish at the other end. That is to say, the starting point was when the logs arrived raw out of the forest; then they were dried in a kiln, sliced up in a log slicer, sliced up further for lumber, treated, tested, coded, glued, trimmed, edged . . . all the way through to the end of the line where they're packed, wrapped, strapped, forked, tossed, trucked and shipped around the world. Find out where the problems were and figure out how to fix them.

For weeks I went around to every single machine and workstation, took copies of all the tools, forms and information used at every stage; talked with every single person along the line about every step they took, what they thought of it, how they liked their job and what issues and ideas they had. Every day I took this information back to a windowless war room in the plant office where an old hand named Des and I would marshall an assemblage of Post-it notes, markers and sticky tape stuck on the huge sheets of brown paper that were covering the four walls end to end. You walked in, opened the door, switched on the yellow light, turned left and saw 'Log Comes In'. Pace around the sheets of brown paper hanging from the walls and every successive step was laid out for everybody to see, ending with 'Trucked to Port'.

This is a map. Who knew then that you could use this idea for anything? It creates your own jigsaw puzzle of the world as you see it today, and then you can climb into it with the ideas and information that you can touch, feel and point to as you walk around it. Just like a Monet, you stand back and see the big picture to take it all in and as you get up close you see the tiny details and flaws or ideas springing to life as they get big enough to see. You can move bits around if you disagree or don't like them any more and put that Post-it note there instead of here, or if you get a better idea you write out another one and stick it where it fits. There was a lot more potential for this brown-paper thing than fixing the Japanese customer's problem with the wood.

I gathered the parts and put them all together. Week by week a holistic picture began to emerge until all the problems stood out like bullet holes on a shot-up van. When we thought we were done, we called an assembly. Every single person from each department could walk through the brown paper cave and critique it or comment on it. Our display had a few knots, but the theory was almost flawless. The trouble was, what worked on paper wasn't working in the pit. The management and heads of department came in after the workers and began pointing the finger at each other's areas.

Problem number one was that nearly every workstation didn't really understand how their part in the chain related to all the others. There was no appreciation for the implications of doing something wrong over here to what ended up over there; or that taking a little longer to do something now had a domino effect later; or how not filling out this form meant wrong inputs on the next.

Problem number two was that people weren't doing what they were meant to do when something went wrong with the system. 'Machine's broken. I just push the wood down the other side instead.'

The problems in the mill were no different from the problems in the wider world and in our lives: if people don't know why they are doing what they're doing they don't have a reason to care; if people don't see how their part affects others and how none of us can live alone they will live only for themselves; and when root causes in ourselves or our world aren't known or break down, we default to fixing the symptoms because it's just too hard to fix the system.

Brown Paper 101 should be mandatory learning around the world — the only thing that should be optional is the colour of the paper. It isn't really the stuff of management consultants and business grads at all — it's common sense. Lay out what you know about something, what you actually have, do and control and how everyone and everything interrelates as it is *today*. Lay it all out as you'd like it to be *tomorrow*. Spot the difference and voilà! You get a framework of how it all should work, how each person sees the world they live in relative to the rest, what's missing and a tool to help fill the gaps. How you fill the gaps is where you get to play magician — the map arms you with the insights to guide you to the right questions to lead you to the right ideas.

Often we struggle the most when we don't see the whole picture — we just see the piece we know best and look outwards from there. The trouble is, although both you and I are standing at 'I Am Here', where you stand depends on where I sit and my Here is not yours and your Here is not mine. We can only project our own assumption-filled interpretations onto the Here of others — every so often, like going to the doctor, everybody should be forced to listen to someone else's version of themselves.

Bringing these pieces together also helped to underscore the vision of the mill. What are all these pieces here to achieve in the first place? How was I to know that such a great life lesson lay dormant under the cover of bark and sawdust in a plant in Kawerau? Every piece must play a part. If anything doesn't, then why is it there? If anything's missing, then why isn't it there? If something doesn't *serve* the vision, it needs to have a very strong reason to exist if indeed it should exist at all.

The one great thing the HR team at Fletchers did was probably the thing they least remember and least cared about. A few months into the role all 10 of us grads were sent on a training course to 'bond'. We were crammed into a room with bright lights, white tiles on the ceiling and a U-shaped classroom set-up, and we were taught about a system to help us architect our lives. I don't think they really believed we were going to use it for *that* purpose — especially not a life without Fletchers in the picture — but it was a box of techniques and tools to be a better person, to set better goals, to build better skills and have better abilities. This kind of carry-on makes people wince a little,

I know. Self-help is for those who need it, and we don't, right?

But this kit . . . it promised to be nothing short of a perfectly formed genie in a beige and navy shoebox, designed for getting what you wanted and becoming who you wanted to become. The instructor started us off small. Actions and goals for the next month, the following one, three and five years, then behind those goals, what you would need to be better at to achieve them, or whether you needed to break the bigger goal down into smaller goals. There was a lot more in that kit because when I got home and opened it, it was stuffed with nine cassette tapes, a booklet and flyers of printed notepads, cards and guides.

'You're on your own now, guys. Today was the first step.' She paused to elevate the sense of occasion. 'What matters now is what you do after you leave this room. Whatever you do, you must work together to keep yourselves on track. If you don't, I can promise you all the hard work that you've done today will fall apart. Now go out there and make it happen!'

Like all good conferences and workshops, after the doors closed that day we never discussed them as a group again. I left the course publicly sceptical but privately curious.

A few months went by. The box sat in the bottom of my cupboard like a glowing orb. I picked it up and studied it suspiciously, piece by piece. As uncool as it was, it had a mysterious attraction. *Managing Goal Achievement*, it was called. *Who* would buy this? *Who* would use this?

'Setting Goals. Planning Strategy. Building Belief. Developing Strengths. Evaluating and Managing Progress.'

Hmm.

This is the type of stuff my brother would make fun of me about. Let's be honest, this is the type of stuff you wouldn't actually tell anybody about. Who needs to do all that? Just get on with life, rip, shit and bust to make it all happen, right?

But it was a good box. When Maya wasn't looking I'd play with it and start doing some of the things it suggested. Set goals. Listen to some tapes. Try to define what I believed in. Create some strategies.

But there was something I didn't understand. We were the freshest kids on the block at work and although we'd been gifted this magic box, I quickly came to doubt that the rest of the 1000 people around us knew anything about it. Or maybe they did but didn't care.

I'd go around asking people casually, 'What are your goals for this year? Next year?' to hear unstructured streams of consciousness or vapid answers like 'I just take it as it comes, man.' A few weeks later I'd try another one over lunch, 'Do you know what you believe in? What are your values?' and be met with blank stares over mince pies. I tried people my age. I tried people twice my age. I tried people in the middle. Same answers. Or no answers at all.

It was all very odd. Why were we given the box when nobody used it? Was it a trap? I used the box to learn about myself. What was I getting better at getting better at? What would I like to add to that story? I decided that ever since I was small I'd got better and better at two things. They were my trademark.

First, when I believed in what I was doing, I *always* tried my best. I went downstairs and I kicked that football against the wall at every different angle hundreds of times an hour. But when I didn't believe in something — like everything that wasn't maths in Form 5 — I did *just* enough to pass. There was never really anything in the middle. It was either crush it or cruise it.

Second, I was never scared to call 'time'. I could pause,

hop in a helicopter in my mind and see the entire landscape of everything that was going on. I could make a tough call to change course if I thought I needed to. Whatever the perceived constraints, rules or frameworks, if I believed there was a better way to achieve the results I needed, then I took the time to stop and try a few things. I created the way that suited me, rather than the other way around.

If there was a third, it was that I asked for permission later. Do it. Then say sorry.

These were good things to know. These ideas became my friends. But I wanted new friends, new skills, new strengths and new ideals to reach for that stretched out much further into the future. The box guided me. We sat down together and I tried to design a life.

Like Brown Paper 101, Life Design 101 should be mandatory. Undesigned lives are lives falling short like birds unknowingly tethered to the ground when they could fly. Without knowing our values and beliefs, we don't know what we stand for. Without a vision we miss a guiding star to pull us through the peaks and troughs. Without goals we can't strive and without plans we can't act. The box convinced me that extraordinary lives need more than a fleeting sense of fate and a dependence on destiny — even fate needs bending and destiny needs dreaming. As it stands, most people's dreams look like the dreams of others and most dreams in the world remain just that, waiting for somebody to have the courage to turn them into reality.

I'm not saying the box was the Oracle of Delphi, but it inspired me never to have that happen to *my* dreams.

Not long after opening the box, courtesy of the very people I'd joined a few months earlier who gave it to me, I used it to set

Sometimes the safe thing to do is the riskiest.

my first goal: to leave my job to start building my own dreams, my own way. Now.

I quit in the closed-off conference room just to the left of the landing by the elevators. There was nothing notable about the room or the occasion, only that it was a short meeting I wasn't looking forward to and one tinged with a strange sadness — I think more due to the milestone of the occasion than the substance of it. My boss Geoff said he thought I really should try it for another six months but when I've made a decision, I generally have the will to see it through.

Soon enough things changed and before my next chapter could even hope to begin, I was living in the purgatory of that $100,000 hole.

05

Anzacs

It's a different kind of prison, being bankrupt — one with bars on freedom, independence and social standing instead of steel bars of physical restraint. A sign hung around my neck, 'This Young Man Didn't Pay His Debts', a shackle chaining me to an assignee, appointed by the court like a parole officer. He wouldn't tell me when to eat or when to exercise but would tell me what I could buy, how much I could spend and take control of my bank accounts and wallet like your mum does when you're 10. I couldn't go overseas without his permission and he'd check that the car I was driving was worth no more than a few thousand dollars, and that the clothes and worldly possessions I owned amounted to not much more. He'd put my name in the paper so that everybody knew exactly what I was.

This picture was simply not an option for me.

I imagined being 22 years old with my whole life ahead of me, having my freedom taken away before I'd even started to know her because of a bed that I'd made. It was not something I was prepared to do. For my family, modest yet proud, bankruptcy would have been crushing, an embarrassing tarnish, all due to a well-constructed if somewhat risky scheme that spiralled a few degrees out of control. I never considered the idea. Perhaps I never had the clarity of thought to imagine it right in those moments, and perhaps I never considered it because it simply wasn't going to be allowed to happen. What I mean, and I think you know what I'm saying, is that it just was *not* a possibility. I would find a way out.

Do you remember Eddy and his mates sitting at the bar in the opening scenes of the movie *Lock, Stock and Two Smoking Barrels*? He'd just lost £100,000 in a poker game with 'Hatchet' Harry Lonsdale and was plotting with his friends how he was going to get out of it — get out, that is, without Harry coming after his old man's pub. Different currency, similar problem.

That afternoon when I hung up from Ray the broker, I reached far and wide across the world in desperation, trying to call in favours from friends and connections who I thought might be able to help. A few thousand here and a few thousand there, it would all add up. Pick up the phone, dial a number, sell my story, hang up, pick up the phone, dial again and again and again. Some of them came through right there on the line with whatever they could, but many didn't even though they had the means. My pitch was really very simple: number one, I'll pay you back; number two, I'll never forget what you did for me and one day I will be in a position where that will count for something. All in all, largely down to a friend called Keiji, I stitched together just enough to stay afloat without calling my parents to let them know what had really happened. It was a call that would have been devastating for all of us and one that I was unwilling to make.

I'd got myself into a scrape, and thank God, with good people, a bit of luck and some creativity, I'd bought some time and dug myself out of it without having to run to Father. That's all I cared about for now. I had bigger things to worry about moving forward.

As the clouds cleared, I looked over my shoulder at the worst possible start to my 'career'. It seemed like a helicopter that had crashed into earth, a carnage of twisted risks and a blackened, burned-out wreck of an idea that I now stepped away from brushing the debris off. I've never thought about my career as distinct from my life, but whatever it was, there could have been no more dangerous way to start one than what I'd just orchestrated for myself. At least I was walking out of it alive.

And as I walked, life went into slow motion for an instant to tell me how lucky I was to have been put through this at 22 and not 42. I was a loser but I felt like I'd won something worth winning. It made whatever problems I thought I had before vanish. Now I knew what a *real* problem was. All I ever heard about people's problems were money, jobs, love and death. I'd just dusted off the worst of the first two and I'd hardly been out in the world for a year.

As the rubble shrank further and further into the distance behind me, something dawned on me one day as I reflected on what I'd just escaped: I was not afraid any more. Of anything.

I was totally void of fear. If *this* was as bad as things would get, then things could only get better. It's hard to say but I think maybe I even felt blessed to have put myself so early on in life to probably one of the greatest tests of pressure. Who would want to be *blessed* by such a nightmare?

'Eating glass and staring into the abyss.' SpaceX and Tesla founder Elon Musk once described being an entrepreneur this way and although I wasn't one yet, it pretty much sums up how I felt. Having just finished the eating, it was now time for the staring. I was physically exhausted but mentally ready. Ready to get up off the mat and ready to start putting one foot in front of the other. Once I knew I'd made it out, I knew I was ready to keep walking.

I had nothing.

I was nobody.

The way I saw it still, with my family, friends and Maya beside me, from here I could become anybody and do anything.

Before I left Fletcher Challenge Forests I had already started thinking about what type of company I might like to build. That thinking reignited with a renewed urgency at the apartment in Anzac Avenue that I shared with Maya and my flatmate Jamie. Jamie McLellan was a designer at Fisher & Paykel, a local company that made dishwashers and washing machines. Maya worked in the Farmers Trading Company headquarters where I'd called her up those weeks before and begged her to come home. Each morning, they went off to work, leaving me alone in the apartment.

Anzac Avenue is a nondescript road in central Auckland that curves up the hill from the waterfront to the university. Our apartment was at 105, at the corner of the bend, and had a lounge that led out to a balcony. I call it a balcony but what it really was, was a line of terracotta tiles which made it *feel* like you were outdoors as you stepped from the carpet, leaving the threshold from the lounge. Two sliding glass doors separated the rectangular space from the lounge inside. My new job was dreaming up a company. I didn't have a boss but I had this balcony.

I was rarely up before nine or ten in the morning and even then my eyes were red. To open them was like prying open a vault — not because I was lazy or sleeping in, but because I had worked through the night before, drinking tea until dawn and was waking up only to do it all over again. It was a gruelling, exhilarating and beautiful thing. I had total freedom and zero accountability or responsibility to anybody other than to find a vision to follow and an adventure to begin. I was on a search for something to light up my heart enough to start. I knew nothing about technology or the internet except enough to know that it was where the action was.

Hour would blend into hour, morning into evening, night into dawn as I researched online, read magazine after magazine and book after book. I might eat a little breakfast but would then forget to eat for the rest of the day and into the night until Maya came home. I'd watch movies and speak to people, analyse business models, ideas and concepts that I thought would give me clues to the future. Before long, the balcony walls were covered with ripped out magazine articles; red, green and black marker on long sheets of brown paper; endless squares of Post-it notes lined up in a colourful mosaic one after another each with a single idea. It looked like a madman's cave — not far off Dr Nash's lab in the movie *A Beautiful Mind*.

As the weeks wore on, dozens of directions and pieces of inspiration from everywhere poured onto the walls, waiting for an idea to spring from them. This was not yet the place or time for specifics — anything was possible, nowhere was off limits and the more directions the better. To give basic structure to the chaos, I used pens of different colours and Post-it pads for different types of thoughts — ideas might be yellow, questions might be green, a statistic or quote might be blue — so when I looked I could instantly see what was where. As I got exhausted from thinking up new things or seeking new energy, I made a cup of tea and stepped away from the sheet-covered walls and glass doors. I walked back from the paper and paced around it so that I could *see* it all in one wide canvas. I stared at it as a whole. I stared at each piece, leaning over to pick up a Post-it note and move it to a better place. I took a marker pen, and drew across the sheets from one idea or piece of information to another with an arrow to show the connection. I consciously observed all of the thoughts mapped out in that universe of ideas.

I digested and dissected each concept one by one across the map of ideas, and then matched the similarities between very different ideas and shared characteristics from the myriad of colours and textures on the walls. I moved things around constantly to try and create order out of the chaos of dozens of thoughts strewn across a room. Little by little, like iron filings huddling towards magnets in different hotspots across the brown paper sheets, patterns started to form. Patterns that represented clusters of ideas that lit up paths of the future that I believed would become reality in five or 10 years.

As I waded through the interconnected maze of possibilities, Christmas came closer and I gravitated towards two clear clusters that in the year 2000 appeared to me to be strong enough visions of how the world might look in the year 2010.

One pattern was the notion of peer-to-peer connections via the internet, creating new types of networks and exchanges out of collections of individual people that were connected together through their computers online. The most obvious example was the idea of the local second-hand marketplace meeting the classified newspaper ads meeting the internet — which became eBay, or a local version in each country like Trade Me in New Zealand or Taobao in China. The exchange gets everybody in one place on the web and lets them use that place as a platform to trade their goods and services while they clip the ticket — but aside from that, the customers are the ones actually doing the work. Brilliant.

Where else was disruption occurring in exchanges? Online stockbroking was starting to take off and although there was still a middle man in the equation (originally the internet was simply used as an order form for the brokers to then enter into the official stock exchange system), it was providing such efficiencies and scale that it was rapidly crushing the previously exorbitant brokerage fees that stockbrokers had become used to charging. A 5 per cent fee quickly became 1 per cent.

Elsewhere, young hacker Sean Fanning and entrepreneur Sean Parker had just created something that threatened to bring down the entire music industry — Napster. Napster was an application that, when downloaded to your computer, allowed you to connect with everyone else who was connected to the Napster network. Once you'd done that you could search an exchange of hundreds of thousands of interconnected computers for the music they had on their hard drives and click to download it from them for free.

Underpinned by the notion of digital exchanges and person-to-person networks, the conditions were ripe to create world-changing, revolutionary new services almost everywhere you looked.

The second pattern bubbling under the surface was the idea of what mobile devices would look like once they collided with the internet. In 2000 a mobile phone was something you talked into and occasionally used to play a black and white game called 'Snake'. SMS was barely in existence; it was initially designed for network engineers to test their systems, not for you and me to send texts to each other. The idea that your mobile phone could be a new, portable form of the internet was gestating. It was clunky, there was no bandwidth, no content and it didn't work at all well. The idea that the internet could live on your phone or that your phone could get things from the internet via SMS had very little credibility as people were simply unable to make it work. What *was* working back then was what people called PDAs — personal digital assistants. You loaded them up with notes and contacts and then brought them back to sync with your computer via a cable. I went out and bought one — a Palm Pilot m100 — the cheapest one I could afford and even then of course I couldn't really afford it at all.

During this discovery period I impulsively started a consultancy service that I called No. 8 Wireless while I was crawling into the future of mobile. In New Zealand, number 8 wire refers to a gauge of fencing wire and has become shorthand for the Kiwi way of being inventive, adaptable and ingenious. As we were moving into a wireless era I thought it was perfect. My first client at No. 8 was also the first person to interview me for my job at Fletchers — Alistair Helm. Shortly after I left, I told him I was looking seriously at the mobile world and would he like a picture painted as to what its implications might be for the business units he was responsible for? In November, while I was still swimming in a sea of brown paper, he became my first client and agreed to a services contract of 80 hours charging $100 an hour to kick off my newfound freedom. My research and recommendations were due to Alistair by early December. In a month I'd transformed my perceived worth from $28,000 a year in the job I'd just left, to $8000 in six weeks in a job I had made up.

After months of working broad brush in big, expansive skies and strokes, over the coming weeks I went very deep and nearly drowned in those two distinct pools of possibility. I bought a simple black A4 notebook with white paper heavy enough to absorb the thick black ink of ideas coming from my pen. I like to draw my ideas rather than write them, so there were no lines on the pages. With this notebook I moved off the walls and onto its small canvas, getting far more specific about what ideas I might embark on within the larger context of these two overarching trends: mobile and connected exchanges.

At university I'd spent a lot of time reading and rereading a book by the management guru Peter Drucker, *Innovation and Entrepreneurship*, where he presented a framework of all the questions he might ask about an opportunity. What's the problem you're trying to solve? What's the new knowledge that makes the solution possible? What are the converging trends of the future that make this achievable?

With nothing but time I set to work. Features flowed freely — in other words, features of a business but not a business model or vision itself. What kind of features? One of the ones I thought was most compelling was wouldn't it be cool if your mobile phone could be turned into a wallet that transmitted wirelessly over the network to pay for small purchases, like your parking at the parking meter?

What about how inefficient it seems when you have an appointment with the hairdresser or the dentist and the receptionist has to pick up the phone, manually call you, incur the 50 cents for connecting to your mobile phone, only to leave a voicemail saying, 'Mr Handley, we look forward to seeing you on Tuesday.' That's annoying, and a waste of money, so what about sending an SMS that I can reply to that automatically updates your patient software database?

What about if you are an owner of a retail store and you want to create a database to let people know about your latest sale? Instead of paying somebody to design and lay out a lovely branded postcard, print everybody's address on it, stick a stamp and then mail it out at 40 cents a pop plus the cost of stationery, what about sending a text to their phone on the very day the sale started instead?

These ideas seemed ridiculously simple. However, they

certainly weren't obvious to anybody I knew. I spoke about them mainly with my friend Keiji, who I'd met at Selwyn College on his first day from Japan after he had convinced his parents to let him move to New Zealand alone at the age of 15. Keiji was now a designer and had a mind all of his own and an insatiable curiosity for the possible, so he became my sparring partner for what might lie ahead. To him, no idea was a stupid one.

We went riffing on this idea of what would happen in physical locations when multiple people had these networked mobile devices. What if three people had an m100 and they were in the same bar? He dreamed up the concept of putting little wireless hotspots on each table that you could choose to connect to, enabling you to chat to people in the vicinity. We mocked it up, and took pictures as if it was a reality for his final-year university project.

Next I tackled the trend of exchanges. I took the framework of online exchanges or peer-to-peer networks, and reverse-engineered the patterns and characteristics that I thought made them work — I was looking for the unique set of conditions that made an exchange a truly compelling answer to a genuine problem in a marketplace or community. What I came up with is a filter, or a lens — a set of criteria that an idea would need to meet to qualify:

- Is there a currently manual or offline method of matching buyer and seller to set a market price? Does this appear inefficient compared to a theoretical digitised process — if one were to exist?
- Is there a marketplace that once built can become the dominant player?
- Is there a product that can be digitally expressed, paid for and received?
- Is there a market of sufficient scale offline that if part of

the marketplace migrates online, there is a big enough share that can be taken?

- Is there a high margin being charged in the market for unnecessary 'friction costs'? Are people getting paid to do things that if an efficient marketplace was built, they wouldn't need to do?
- Will distributing the market more widely and attracting more people to the network make the market more and more efficient and attractive for the participants? As this gets bigger does it automatically become better, cheaper or faster for the consumer?
- Can the market be created simply through the efforts of the market participants themselves? Do they create the product and services (not the company providing the platform)?

Those were the characteristics I saw as necessary to possibly turn an industry upside down and on its head. I then searched through this lens to find things that fitted. I didn't have far to look. Remember back when I was at school, I spent a lot of time investing my money in the sports-betting market and determined that the bookmakers who were setting the odds were taking far too high a margin? Bingo.

Was there an inefficient offline method for setting the price of the goods? Yes. The price of the goods was the odds people were offered when making a bet; the method of setting it was done manually in sports betting by a bookmaker who looks at the statistics and determines the chances.

Was betting on sports and the races a big market? Billions. Was there a product that could be digitally transacted? There's nothing physical about a bet — a bet is just a memory backed up with honesty. Can a marketplace be created whereby the market participants create the 'content', i.e. the betting odds? In an exchange all the customers would set their own odds online — you would just have to create the software platform that enables them to do so and to digitally record the bet and then move the money to the winner when it had been won.

In short, the answers to all the questions as to whether sports betting was a market ripe for disruption by creating a person-to-person exchange — much like a stock exchange for stocks; a marketplace where the people who want to make the bets get to set the odds and do it themselves, between each other — were the right ones.

All up there must have been a hundred other ideas in that black A4 notebook. All it took to paint visions of the future — many of which might come true — was my fledgling courage and conviction; my red, green and black marker pens; my Post-it notes and papered walls; my books, my magazines and my internet; all it took was my imagination in vivid colours and intensity of effort, a little help from a few friendly frameworks and friends who liked playing make-believe.

I had two strong ideas that had yet to be translated into a tangible plan or business.

To make sure I wanted to do what I was about to do I created one last filter — a set of lenses to validate two values I hold dear. Two simple questions: if I do this, do I believe I can be among the best in the world at it? And if I do it, is it going to be really, really difficult? That way, even if I fail, I would learn infinitely more than if I tackled something easier. It would have to be something so big that it was worth trying and failing for.

Absolutely nobody I knew was starting a tech company, so I tried to hunt out and cold-call possible mentors. I sent handwritten notes asking for just a few minutes to meet for a coffee to share some tips and words of wisdom before I stepped into the abyss. Mostly I never heard back — I did get a reply from one person but she never actually agreed to meet with me and eventually stopped replying. I gave up on the search and just went for it alone.

When it came to software, I didn't know anything about that either, but I couldn't see how that could possibly matter. I would find people who did.

There was just one more phase I went through before I locked myself into either direction, which was to share, conceptually, what I was about to embark on with friends and associates for feedback. I had a few close confidants — Jamie, Keiji — who were part of the internal dialogue process but I needed to go wider and gauge reactions. This didn't go down so well. It wasn't so much an outright backlash or running down of my character or spirit as much as a lack of interest and belief.

My brother Geoffrey was still in a job at this time, but he was starting to get really intrigued by the possibilities ahead of us and was tempted to jump ship and join the journey. We had two trends before us — two opportunities both as unpredictable and as impossible as the other, but both potentially enormous. Given our experience in each of these areas — which was practically nothing — each looked as ridiculous on paper as the other. We had to just choose one. I was feeling the heat to pick a path and get things moving, but couldn't decide.

I called my parents up one day to test them out. We had lunch and I brought them round to the brown-paper cave in Anzac Avenue. I sat them down to tell them what I had been doing and to paint this picture of what might be created in the years to come. I ended with, 'This device,' holding the Palm m100 out towards them, 'this is the precursor to devices that will change the way we do everything. I'm not sure what *everything* means but I am pretty sure that this thing here is what I'll be building some kind of a business on.'

'Well, I've had these types of devices for the last few years — they don't work very well — but I'm sure you're heading in the right direction on something,' Dad said in one of his gentler tones.

Mum didn't say too much and that was about it. They didn't seem overly inspired. It was the first time I'd sat my parents down and tried to tell them what I thought the future looked like. Not tomorrow, not next year but the future three, five or 10 years out. Actually it might have been the first time I authentically tried to sit anyone down and have them believe I knew what the future might look like.

They didn't give me a steer and as it got closer to Christmas, Geoffrey and I knew we had to pull the trigger on *something*. We decided, screw it, let's start both companies and see what happens. Neither of us knew what to expect, nor how long it would take for us to find out. One thing we knew was that many years earlier Dad had chosen to eat glass and leap into the darkness of the abyss. So would we.

Faith is taking the first step even when you don't see the whole staircase.

Martin Luther King Jnr

06

Feverpitch

Feverpitch. That's what we decided to call the betting business. I entered a phase where I was more obsessed than anything I have been obsessed with before. It became my life.

From everything I'd read about starting a start-up, the first thing to do once you had a vision was to come up with a plan; once you had a plan you had to create a story; once you had a story you had to use it to raise money to make it a reality. Once you have some money, you really begin.

I put together my story, a collection of pieces strung together for about 15 minutes to convince somebody to give me money they had worked very hard to earn in exchange for a small piece of my company. The story starts with either the market or the idea, then goes on to the plan and the team. I put mine together in a PowerPoint presentation with a light grey background and crimson font.

I gave my first presentation to John, a potential investor who also happened to be Maya's dad. He was involved in a drug company start-up that had just listed publicly on the NASDAQ stock exchange in New York.

We sat at his dining-room table and I put the laptop on the tablecloth. My story opened with, 'P2P is the New Network — Feverpitch is Napster meets Ebay meets the TAB'. It was rubbish.

I'm not young enough to know everything.

Oscar Wilde

The presentation was full of jargon and utterly meaningless. I was still in an echo chamber of my own thoughts and imaginary friends I'd met through the magazines, websites and stories I was reading. I had forgotten how to speak and write English. John's blank face was a wake-up call. I regrouped, translated myself back into English and went back on the roadshow again to pitch for dough. I loved it. This was a chance to pitch an impossible dream and convince people to come along for the ride. I hadn't quite appreciated just how much of a stretch Feverpitch was for people to latch on to — the concept of online betting was hard enough for most people to grasp, let alone the idea of shaking up the industry through a model where people would bet against each other through an online exchange.

Dad gave us introduction after introduction to people who had money and were willing to take a punt on crazy schemes. A few of them became believers and came aboard, either because they got it, or because they were scared that if they didn't get it, they'd miss out on the next big thing. The more you tell the story, the better you get at it. The more people ask questions, the more you bake the answers into the story so that next time by the end of the 15 minutes there are very few questions left to answer. This was the selling I loved: selling the vision of a company and an idea that didn't exist. And it worked. By early January, through knocking down as many doors as possible and telling them the story, I was up to about $250,000, which was exactly what I had budgeted to take us through the first year of expenses. Boom. Off to the races.

I thought investors should get a third of the company. I had nothing to go on and nobody to ask, but from what I'd read that seemed about right at this early stage. I split the rest of the shares. Geoffrey had not yet committed to joining full time and so he got 15 per cent, my father got 10 per cent for helping us set it all up, Hubert (a friend who had helped research ideas from England) got 5 per cent and I got the rest — about 40 per cent. It wasn't lost on me was that if the investors' $250,000 was worth 30 per cent of the company, then my 40 per cent must have been notionally worth at least a bit more than that.

Every week we had a meal at Gina's. A small, cheap and chic Italian restaurant on Symonds Street not far from the office, Gina's had an open kitchen down the entire length of the room filled with loud young Italians with white T-shirts and bandanas singing through the service area. With my friends, I was deliberately reserved and vague about my plans — not because I had fear of people stealing the idea, but because I was very reluctant to set up expectations of something without being able to deliver. I passionately disliked it when people spoke about their latest incredible adventure or idea and then just a few months later they were onto a new thing as if the previous one had never existed. In those early weeks I just said I was starting an internet company and I hoped to be able to explain it better soon. I am not a fan of unnecessary mystery but some people might call me aloof. It's not aloofness for the sake of being stand-offish; it's more to do with not being willing to share something I am working on until I am confident that it will indeed happen and has a reasonable chance of success.

Many meals would pass at Gina's where people would have no real clue as to what I was working *so* hard on that I could barely stay awake at the dinner table. One night, I do remember thinking about how I went from almost being bankrupt a few months ago to being worth $300,000 (on paper at least) in a company that didn't yet exist, and wanting desperately to talk about the ridiculousness of the idea. I wanted to ask, 'Why don't they teach you this magic at school?'

Things were on a roll. With some money in my bag, I now needed some people. Geoffrey was not going to be ready for a few months so I thought of one of my university friends who might be just mad enough to see this as a journey he wanted to take. I called him up — he was still in Wellington where we'd been studying — and unloaded a stream of consciousness on him.

'Hey Pete, how's it going? What are you up to? Are you a lawyer yet? Got a job yet? No, don't do that. That'll be boring.

'I'm starting this business and it's in online gambling — er, yeah, but I'm going to create an exchange on the internet — yeah, kind of like eBay but not quite — and people will go on, and one person will say, I think the Hurricanes are going to lose so I'll bet against them and I want odds of 2–1 and I'll wait for somebody else to come along and bet against them.

'What?

'No I don't know how to build it — that's not why I'm calling you — yeah, so they'll come on, they'll bet against each other and then we'll get a cut.

'Do we have a licence? No, of course not. The TAB has the only licence. But look, this is the internet and there are no rules on the internet, *we make the rules*, and maybe it's not even gambling. We are just facilitating betting between the two parties. We are a facilitator, maybe we're not even an operator?

'We'll figure out all of that later. I've got some Indian partners to develop it. So what I'm saying is, do you want to come up as I have a job for somebody to help set this up. Somebody to build this community and help create the markets for these rugby bets. I want it to be up and running for the start of the Super 12 season in February 2001.

'Next week? Yes, come up next week. Right. See you.'

I'd picked the right guy. Someone spontaneous enough

to just get on a plane, move city and join a journey with no idea where it might start or end. We put ourselves on salaries of about $35,000 and began. It was January, and the rugby season started in February. I thought we'd build this entire online exchange in two months. I thought Feverpitch would be a success and I'd be out of there within two or three years, a millionaire many times over. I had no idea.

I hunted around for the cheapest place to get an office, somewhere close to my apartment because I expected lengthy late nights. Within a few weeks I found one just down the road at 80-something Anzac Avenue. It was the top floor of a very old and poorly kept building — to find it, I just walked into building after building and wandered around to see if there was anything available. I took the lift to the fourth floor, walked up two flights of stairs to what looked like an abandoned level and poked around. There were several small, unlocked offices but nobody there. I asked around for the landlord's phone number, paid a $5000 deposit and we had a room for a year at around $200 a week that could fit about six of us, eight at a stretch. The torn carpet was a faded blue. The air conditioner didn't work and it was unbearably hot with the sun shining down on the roof. We split the room into two areas, one for all the workstations and the other for a meeting table. I gave Keiji $250 to build us a table, some shelves and some storage cupboards. This was our new home.

Relentless and possessed. There aren't two better words in the English language to describe how we operated. I could not focus on *anything* else for more than a few minutes — my mind was nowhere but on the business and the things that needed to be done that day, week and month. If there was a meal to be had, there was no longer any social element to it — it was merely to refuel my energy to get back to the work of building this company, designing this software and launching to the market. If there was a conversation going on, it was simply white noise to rest my mind as an interlude before going back into battle. I was physically present but mentally absent to my family and friends. Just let me work hard, finish this company, and I'll rejoin the real world when I'm done. I promise.

Every night we would work until our eyes were red, dry and begging us to shut them. In those early days we would rarely head home before 10 or 11 at night, only to reunite at seven or eight in the morning, and for the first year or two it was almost always seven days a week. My understanding was that it took commitment like this to succeed.

With the money we had, we got to work. I knew nothing about software other than what I'd learned in the preceding months, I'd never even met a software developer and I'd never built a product for the internet. We started anyway. My brother knew of an Indian outfit that had just set up shop in Auckland and before we knew it we had a team of about 10 technologists in Visakhapatnam, Andhra Pradesh in southern India on our payroll that we communicated with every day and night via internet chat and emails.

Every evening, as our exhaustion tilted towards collapse, we pulled out two blank CDs for our last ritual of the evening and put them in the disk drive of our Hewlett Packard home PC that we'd bought on hire-purchase for $30 a week. We began to copy the entire contents of our files from the computer onto the disks. This process would take a while, and we watched as all the file names transferred over, the disk drive whirred, stuttered and spun and eventually stopped. Either Peter or I pulled out the disk, scrawled 'Back up', and the date and time on it with a red marker and ran off home with it so that if the office burned down or got broken into, all was not lost. The disks from this well-thought-through plan to ensure continuity should disaster strike piled up over the months. It took us a long time to realise that we had never backed up a single thing — all that we had done was the first step. When the disk stopped whirring at the end of those cold dark nights, it had merely written the file structure and was waiting for us to click the 'Burn' button to actually copy the files. Who knew? Not us, we knew nothing about software and computers.

We dedicated every waking hour in a race to exist, to launch and to take our fascinating idea to the world. Convinced that competition was bearing down on us from unknown quarters we were in a race against the clock with what little money we had raised. We were burning cash and always needed more — we couldn't afford to do anything right but kept pushing ahead anyway. We built the product, rebuilt it, and even built a version that could be used to make bets, check your account and deposit money through the internet on your mobile phone.

While Peter focused on preparing the systems and processes for the betting markets, I focused on the development of the product and preparing for future capital raising. Within a year the company was ready to list on what was basically a new ventures board of the New Zealand Stock Exchange for small high-growth companies, and by February 2002 the ticker FVR was trading. All of a sudden we were in the media and open for public scrutiny as the youngest kids to sell shares to the public on the stock exchange. We had a bit more money but it wasn't enough. It was never enough.

My personal reputation — not that I had one, and not that I

minded that much what it might be, given the years of life left in me to repair any damage — was now at risk, exposed to the whims of ignorant or doting media. Now that we were in the public eye, we were being watched as we either rose with the challenges or fell with them. One of the sad things about people is that no matter what journey you are trying to make, you can be sure to find those who want to take you down. I had read about this before — in New Zealand we call it the tall poppy syndrome — the depressing thing is that many poppies aren't even that tall yet before people start cutting them down. The true tall poppies have grown a thick skin. It was the early days of internet chatrooms, and I'd log on to see vicious attacks on me. These attacks on a young kid barely out of university were always hidden behind pseudonyms and anonymous online usernames. I learned to roll with the punches and have rolled with them since, as the attacks and put-downs might slow, but they never seem to stop.

It is unbelievable to think things could happen this fast. When you put your mind to something so intently, you convince everybody around you that if there was any way at all for your dream to come true, it will. Sometimes it feels as if everything in the universe conspires to help push you along. Some people call this 'the zone' or 'flow' and we were in it for about a year. While you hope it lasts forever, I can tell you it doesn't and it didn't.

After having decided on America as our target market, the US government started taking significant steps to outlaw all forms of online betting; we shifted our strategy to Australia and not long after started getting letters from the federal government proposing fines of $10,000 a day if we persisted; I spent a lot of time in Las Vegas and Costa Rica trying to sell our software to wise guys and ex-mafia bookmakers all fleeing the US to set up shop in 'legit' offshore locations like Curacao and Antigua.

I met a colourful collection of characters — as I was blazing a trail, with one of the very few software platforms in the world that enabled people to bet against each other on *anything*, anybody would take a meeting with me to have a look at it. I remember most clearly going to visit an Englishman in an eight-storey building in San José, Costa Rica, filled with hundreds of his staff. He had spent his life on the legitimate side of the track, moving up through the ranks of the British betting legend Ladbrokes, the largest bookmaker in England, and had eventually risen to the top as the CEO of BetonSports, Costa Rica, which he built to a billion-dollar company and listed on the London Stock Exchange. He fought hard, and dangerously above the parapet, for legalising the industry, pushing for the government to regulate and tax it, for licences that would enable what was currently below the radar to be public and accountable. Governments sometimes have no clue and would sooner apply prohibition-era thinking than common sense to contemporary widespread human behaviour. This chap ended up in jail when the United States decided it was illegal to accept online bets from its citizens from an offshore jurisdiction.

The sector was one of the fastest-growing in the online world and enormous public companies were being floated on the London Stock Exchange throughout those early years. Unfortunately, as fast as it may have been growing and welcomed in the UK, it was getting banned and attacked by governments around the world even faster. At 24 I was starting to get uncomfortable with how the legitimate side of sports betting (which existed in New Zealand, Australia and the United Kingdom) was overlapping with the shady side (which was largely fuelled by the United States government's abolitionist policy).

The months wore on and the impossible idea — Feverpitch

— was, well, proving to be just that. Everywhere we turned, turned on us; our increasing experience was exposing our inexperience; our limited network was reaching its limits and in an industry that to all intents and purposes was essentially run by gangsters, replays of *The Godfather* were only getting us so far. All the while we continued to bleed cash.

We failed to raise the millions of dollars we needed. We tried to find it in every market from Hong Kong to London but every market was cracking down on the industry before our plane had even touched down. Whatever we did, there just never ever seemed to be enough cash to do it properly.

To compound the money woes, the product we'd built, well it wasn't cutting it. I mean, it was a product, it worked — but to be frank, it was shit. It was always playing catch-up. And our team? Marginally better than the product. We just weren't of the calibre needed to navigate one of the most complex and treacherous industries in the world at a time of tumultuous change and with an idea of such potential disruption — oh, and by the way, build a company from scratch at the same time. In hindsight, I couldn't have picked a more volatile, dangerous and difficult adventure as my first attempt at creating the future.

Starting Feverpitch was always going to open us up to ridicule. On paper, it was an entirely ridiculous notion that we could achieve what we were setting out to achieve. That's why we started it. Maybe Feverpitch was more about the fact that it would be so damned difficult to succeed.

It didn't matter. By late 2002, barely making it to its second birthday, Feverpitch was as dead as a dodo. As soon as it had begun, it was the beginning of the end.

Feverpitch did give me something — the validation that I really could spot patterns. As a vision, as an idea, it wasn't dumb.

The problem was its execution and timing. When we began there were two competitors globally — each had raised tens of millions of dollars — one bought the other and went on to become one of the most successful online businesses in the world, worth billions and billions of dollars.

So we went out to bat based on the right insights and the right forecasts. The journey was built on the right foundations — it was the rest that faltered and failed. As I closed the books on Feverpitch I thought to myself, 'Next time the idea may not be as strong, but I'm going to *execute* the heck out of it so even I can't fault myself on that front.'

Did I have it in me? I would find out soon enough.

What you can gain from experience over the years, you can risk losing in courage, curiosity and freedom. There are things you might not do tomorrow because you are more 'experienced' and think you know better than you do today, yet they would be absolutely the right thing to do. In getting older, and gaining daily in that experience, I figure there are two traits worth fighting to hold on to.

The first is to retain the mind of a child. Youth, Robert Kennedy once said, is not a time of life but a state of mind. Youth, the state of mind, frees us up to avoid letting past experience dictate current thought. Experience is often *wrong*. It is an indicator, not a predicator; an accumulation of the past, not a message from the future — and as situations change, so does the value of experience.

The other is to feel the fear and do it anyway. Ideas are worthless without the courage to bring them to life, and without a sound idea, there's no point being bold about it.

Would I do Feverpitch again? Can't say. But as we got deeper

Experience is only half of experience.

Goethe

into it, I started to doubt that it was something I really wanted and whether it was what I wanted to stand for in the world. Whether it was what my head or my heart wanted me to start — after all, it wasn't so far removed in concept from those trading jobs at BNZ and Macquarie, was it? The universe told me there was something more, some place out there that was uniquely mine to stand on. I wasn't anywhere close to it, but with each step forward and each mistake, lesson or learning, I was getting closer.

Through all the useless reports and information on the sharemarket I'd read as a kid, I knew that there was a way to actually make use of a company like ours that was dying on the stock exchange. Another business could use what assets remained — whatever cash it had left and its status as a publicly listed company. It was kind of like an escape hatch, to use the listed company and turn it into something else. So I looked for what the phoenix that could arise from these ashes might be and soon enough arranged for Feverpitch Limited to acquire a group of childcare companies, bought them by issuing millions and millions of dollars of new shares in Feverpitch and changed the name to Kidicorp. In March 2003 we packed down Feverpitch and up popped Kidicorp — there's nothing as natural as a transition from gambling to childcare — which became a listed company without having to go through the ordeal of an Initial Public Offering and roadshow. Despite its awful name (which it retains to this day) the company has gone on to become the largest childcare operator in New Zealand, with hundreds of millions in revenue, 250 centres, serving almost 15,000 children under the leadership of the very same man we did that deal with, 10 years ago.

Somewhere along the way, based on that little black

book with a hundred ideas on the future of mobile, we changed the working name of No. 8 Wireless to The Hyperfactory and incorporated it in July 2001. It existed to turn those ideas into reality. Lots of ideas, pumped out at hyper-speed. Our logo was a neon-blue old-school factory with smoke stacks and floating halos designed by Jamie. As a gift for their loyalty we rolled our original backers into The Hyperfactory at no extra cost so they would get another roll of the dice. About a year or so earlier my brother Geoffrey had left Feverpitch and transitioned full time to The Hyperfactory with a school friend of mine who came to help us set up our computers when he wasn't at his night job parking cars.

So for the months leading up to March 2003 when the merger with Kidicorp was to take place, Pete and I were the only two staff left at Feverpitch. We spent most nights at the bars in central Auckland racking up bills with my cousin Dan and as many friends as were willing to join us. This was all thanks to the credit cards charging the few thousand bucks left in the Feverpitch tin; I had to spend it before we closed the Kidicorp deal or we'd lose it anyway. Inspired by the wisdom of George Best, I thought we might as well drink it away before the handover and it became what I eventually called my 'birth month' — a simultaneous tribute to the death of Feverpitch and four-week celebration of my birthday. I like a Manhattan — a few drops of Angostura bitters swirled around a martini glass, half bourbon, half sweet vermouth chilled like the Arctic and served up with three cherries. I'd walk into the Crow Bar and they'd have the Manhattan up before I'd got to the stool. I'd drink Manhattan after Manhattan after Manhattan until I couldn't see any more, or couldn't talk any more or just couldn't drink any more.

A few weeks later I decided to escape, to cut and run around the world to explore what I might find, learn and become. I was 25.

I spent a lot of money on booze, birds and fast cars. The rest I just squandered.

George Best

07

Wilderness

I had over $1 million in cash and Kidicorp shares, little debt and no idea what to do with it.

It was March 2003 and I'd spent the last two years so focused on Feverpitch, which had gone up like a little rocket and spiralled down in flames. At least that's how I remember it. On paper it looked very different. In reality it reminded me of the days of dialling Ray the broker, crouched down on that beige carpet in my Anzac Avenue meltdown. Except this time it was a twisted combination of having failed to make an idea happen, but succeeding in making a small bundle of money through the idea's demise. For 25, I was 'rich' but I couldn't feel it. I didn't feel it. It wasn't meant to feel this way — where was the elation? The satisfaction? The I-told-you-so? There wasn't much. At least, I couldn't find it.

I had no place to be; no people to lead; not even a reason to work. I had no Mount Impossible to climb. No vision to paint. I could have lived out my twenties in some semi-retired state, free to not try. It was a dangerously bleak sort of freedom.

You see, Feverpitch itself had flopped — that much I've made clear. But in engineering the merger to create Kidicorp, I'd clipped the ticket and turned the dying dream into a small fortune. Off the back of it we bankrolled The Hyperfactory too.

The Hyperfactory, out there telling people they needed it to teach them how to use technology and ideas to share their brands, companies and messages with people through these little things called mobile phones. It was humming along OK, with Geoffrey out in front, but for now I wasn't interested.

So what about me? Really I preferred not to think about it but not thinking about things never lasts too long.

I had no idea.

I can only tell you that I still felt like a failure. A let-down. A let-down who was drinking too much. I had been caught on a floating platform between two revolving doors, one that had just closed shut and one that I was trying to time myself into. I have a high tolerance for trying things and for risking failure, but that's very different from *wanting* to fail and being OK with it. My body and mind called out for direction and distraction, posing fresh questions but presenting no shortlist of obvious answers: How am I going to come out of this? How am I going to build from here? How am I going to really hit the big time? How am I going to be rich enough to do whatever I want for the rest of my life? How am I going to be a *success*? What they lacked in urgency, the questions made up for in gravity. What was going to be my next move? And why?

When you can do *anything* one mistake to make is to just dive in and do *everything*. For now, I thought I'd just breathe in the world.

Life slows down here for a moment, and so does this story. You'd slow down too if you had nowhere to be. I suppose I could skip this part but you'd be missing out on pieces of me that you might want to know about so they don't become pieces of you.

I'd just survived a fast trip that was so ridiculous it was over before it'd begun, only to find myself right back at the bottom again with no plans or purpose. Ever in search of what destiny had marked out for me, I took off for a wander with no fixed date of return to plot my way around the world, picking out cities from east to west, before the next plunge.

Aside from books of ideas, I had never actually kept a journal — you know, the type where you carve your deepest thoughts; the type you tape mementos and ephemera in that prove you were there and you did those things; the type that becomes the home for your goals and plans for an amazing incredible life that will play out before you. I had never had one and I thought I needed to. So I looked around for something simple, classic and timeless that would grow with my growth, and found it in a Moleskine. These small, black, nameless notebooks claim that artists and thinkers like van Gogh, Hemingway and Oscar Wilde were thought to have used them. If they were good enough for those characters, I figured they must be good enough for me.

A few weeks later my Moleskine, my tiny black Delsey suitcase and I landed in Tokyo's Narita airport. Keiji had moved back to Japan by now and in a typical gesture he came all the way to pick me up; we rattled on the subway back to his split-level shoebox in the Nakameguro district. Upstairs was about a metre in height and wide enough for a single man to sleep; downstairs, it was high enough to stand and long enough for a one-and-a-half-person couch that only the Japanese could make, resting alone about a metre in front of a 14-inch television. I slept on that couch. Keiji went to work each morning and like every young Japanese man climbing his way to the top he had to put in long hours, leaving me to my own devices until dark.

For the first time, I was in a place entirely void of any English that might help me navigate my surroundings. Every Japanese school kid is taught basic English but because the Japanese are so shy and afraid of making mistakes, none of them will speak it; in nearly every major city around the world English appears where you most need it, but not here. I traversed the subway by recognising patterns in the characters and mapping my way through; I ordered food in little cafés with vending machines featuring pictures of meals on buttons. I'd push a button to make my choice; out spat a ticket and I walked up to redeem my lunch, without saying a word. In Tokyo you can vend your way through life and never have to interact with a human being.

Tokyo gave me an unadulterated combination of dis-comfort and ignorance; of being unable to talk or hear but still see and listen, wandering one of the most chaotic, crowded cities in the world, deaf to the conversations around me and entirely alone. The private silence within the public cacophony of Tokyo was perfect.

In the evenings Keiji and I would go to sake bars, drink too many shots and stumble home drunk taking in late-night okonomiyaki pancakes or yakitori sticks from a hole in the wall on our way back to the shoebox. We would stumble in and take off our coats, hanging them on the hangers in white plastic coats to keep out the smell of smoke. Apart from things like coats in coats, we didn't talk about anything important. Keiji isn't really a businessperson, but he understood that Feverpitch was dead. He didn't go into it though, and I didn't really want to talk about any of that anyway.

In the daytime I'd walk around, see the sights, hear the sounds and look at the shops, buildings and people; I chased down buildings by Tadao Ando, my favourite architect, that were scattered around the city, wondering what I might glean from seeing them in reality. I figure there are clues to more than you think within the thinking behind the things that you love.

Tadao Ando's work is created by the intersection of masses of pure, unadulterated grey concrete and the voids they create. It lives through the interplay of the shadows and trapping of light and in his world there *is* no façade — the honesty of the raw materials becomes the austere, serene surface itself. I couldn't get much from wandering around the outside of small buildings that I'd seen revealed naked in the pages of my books — but if this type of purity and order was what I loved in architecture, what did it say about what I needed to architect for my *self*? Since turning 15, I had collected a litany of fearless and naïve attempts, a series of small scrapes and bruises, a few small wins and two catastrophes. I had never been more ready to map something out that guaranteed the life I wanted to live would *actually* happen.

Tokyo was the first stop on a journey of discovery, except there was no discovering happening there. It was more a preparatory loosening up. Stretches before the big match. A week after I'd arrived in Narita I headed to Europe, staying in London and Paris. Thanks to the good grace of some patient friends I landed on couches, not knowing when I'd leave. Weeks blurred into months.

In Paris I first stayed at my friend Vinnie's in the eighteenth district. I got very good at ordering a *carnet* (a packet of subway tickets) so I had to speak less French. I'd take a ticket from my carnet and subway around to meet people and see things. In Paris I met Linlee. Linlee always had interesting things in her bag and during one of our afternoon coffees in a tiny sidestreet café she took out her notepad and a scrap of paper with what looked like a long handwritten list.

'I've begun to ask people these questions?' she ventured.

'Sure—'

'Question one, what is your idea of perfect happiness?'

A long pause.

'I don't know,' I replied.

'Question two, what is your greatest fear?'

'I don't know. Well, no, I think it's somebody I love dying. Maybe it's that.'

'What is the trait you most deplore in others?'

'I would never use the word deplore but a trait I don't like? Well it might be cowardice; or when people say they will do something and they don't. I don't know what you call that.'

'I'm not sure, but it's the opposite of integrity. What is your current state of mind?' she carried on.

'Quiet. Peaceful. Searching?'

'What is your most marked characteristic?'

I looked down at the table, then down the row of tables, and then down the street. I had no idea.

'Who is your hero of fiction?'

I realised I'd hardly read any fiction. I was stuck on the word 'hero' and could only think of Batman and Superman. I'd read hundreds of biographies but I could count on one hand the novels I'd finished. Was that a good thing? I wondered.

'What's the quality you most like in a man? In a woman?'

Uncomfortable silence before I proffered something that I thought might have been the right answer. Surely I've thought about all of these things, haven't I?

'Which talent would you most like to have? What do you regard as the lowest depth of misery? What do you most value in your friends?'

'I don't know . . .'

I stumbled on every response and wondered about each

question, many of which I knew I'd never been asked.

The last questions were the most striking. 'How would you like to die?' And a call to summarise your entire philosophy to life into a battle cry: 'What is your motto?'

I need a motto? Well, I guess my schools all had mottos. And my favourite football teams have mottos. But I don't remember being told *I* needed a motto. I'd never thought about questions like this. For each of them there seemed to be a set of obvious possible answers, a set of immediate gut reactions or 'right answers' — but none of those answers were *mine*, just as none of the questions were Linlee's.

The questions were called the Proust Questions, I found out later. Marcel Proust was a French writer from the early twentieth century, most famous for his novel *Remembrance of Things Past*. Questions that everybody should meet in their life at least once, triggering a revealing array of layers that peel back who we are and how we see the world. One by one they dripped out into the Parisian air that day, prising ever wider the gulf between the things I *thought* I knew and the very many things I had simply never thought about but now felt compelled to. Half-built bridges led off in every direction from my mind and I couldn't follow them all at once.

I decided that the right kinds of answers to these kinds of questions needed to be eased into — they needed to be considered and honest and to come from someplace real; they would take time. I immediately wrote them all down. Every other day I wrote everything else down in my Moleskine too and wandered through the calmness of the Tuileries gardens; I sat on the steel green seats scattered around the fountains and throughout the chalky, dusty paths. I'd write, read, draw or watch — I had no agenda, and nowhere to be.

When I was 10 I'd been to a Picasso exhibition and had never forgotten it. I started to spend a lot of time at the museum in his honour in the Marais area and bought a stack of books on him to keep me company; books on his life, not his art. To study an artist's life is to study their phases and periods — the blue, the cubism, the bulls and all the women who stepped in and out of his paintings as they stepped in and out of his life. 'Every child is an artist, the problem is how to remain an artist once we grow up,' he said. Picasso did this through the continual reinvention of who he was — the ends of old beginnings merging into the beginning of new ends — but all strung together in one long thread of spiritual integrity and consistently characteristic Picasso.

In those same books by the management thinker Peter Drucker, he said that to be innovative was to make your *own* innovations and competitive advantages obsolete before your competitors do. That idea, applied to life itself, and the idea of the life of an artist seemed one and the same. Perhaps I liked the idea of curating such an ideal, where every new act serves to make the previous act stale and passé; perhaps I wanted to be as prolific as Picasso (one of the most prolific artists ever to have lived); perhaps I wanted to create the freedom to reinvent and step in and out of phases, eras and genres; perhaps I wanted to live like an artist?

08

Napoleon

The days in Europe were beginning to open up and the expanses of space and air encouraged me to plot and plan, to let ideas be born and simmer away before putting them back into a bottle with a label and directions. Some space too, to reflect on the last three years.

By London I had etched my first bits and pieces towards a philosophy on life. I wrote a few words on what it might be all about, and tested it on a friend one evening. 'Here's where I've got to so far.'

She paid attention for long enough to not have to pay attention to anybody else in the tiny flat.

'We visit places. We collect experiences, relationships and things,' I started.

'I don't collect my life,' she stopped me.

'Well, if you're not collecting, what are you doing? Just letting things happen to you? I don't think that's how we live. We are purposeful, so we collect the things we want in life. Maybe it sounds calculated but collect is as good a word as any.'

'What if I don't have a plan and I just work towards a direction?'

'Somewhere among it all, goals and a plan need to happen or you will never get it all done. To bend fate, you need plans. To

Bad artists copy. Good artists steal.

Picasso

plan, you need goals. To create goals, you need to know what you want to collect.'

'A plan is better than no plan,' she agreed.

'The world's a big place — how much of it do you want to make a part of you? *Where* do you want to be? You make visits and create presence, collecting the pieces you want and building relationships and friendships along the way. I mean that as you travel, thought and place become intertwined — thoughts and ideas become attached to place. To put down mental and physical roots around the world, I want presences — countries, cities, homes, beaches or museums.

'There's more. Inner attributes, qualities and skills — *who* do you want to be? To make the most out of all of this time we have, to always be better and learning and trying. Who do you want to be known as? The things you believe in and can do? Generosity, passion, creativity; languages, music, art, talents?'

A few cups of tea but no real answers. So far, that was it. The sum total of the journey of what I knew about life was basically those paragraphs, drawn from a quarter-century of trying my best to live my best. I wrote it down word for word in a naïve, mildly precocious and entirely simplistic manifesto. To be perfectly frank, it's not missing too much — but what it *is* missing are the perfect parts that would take me a few more years to learn. What I took to be important (and what I still take to be important) is that I had started to shape something — the outlines in a child's colouring book, the purposeful architecture of the pieces I thought I needed to create the life I want to live. Who knew what the pieces were? Least of all me. That I'd started, I took to be a milestone; that it was imperfect, I took for granted.

I began to colour it in, and for this I looked to what I could remember of the magic box I'd been given at Fletcher Forests; I borrowed from the Proust Questions and sprinkled in others to create a hybrid of the various development methodologies and philosophies I'd come across that helped to define who I wanted to become and what I wanted to achieve. But most of all, I lent on a peculiar and unique voice, the unpretentious, earnest conversation of Napoleon Hill, who spoke to me through a book he'd written in 1937 called *Think and Grow Rich*.

You might have heard of it, maybe you haven't. It's one of the biggest-selling titles in history and has sold over 70 million copies; it's the precursor to all the books today that try to teach you how to be who you want to be. He wrote of richness in the broadest sense and with so much detail and so many questions that in my copy it's easier to find the pages that *aren't* bookmarked or cornered over than it is to find the ones that are. The colouring in became a conversation with Napoleon Hill in my head, with his turns of phrase peppered with the folksy tones of his era. He'd speak through the printed words and instruct me one after the other: 'Write down what you want to be. Write down what you want to have. What are you going to give in return, because nothing comes for free. And above all, what you need is a *definiteness* of purpose — something to stand for and dedicate your life to.'

At his urging, I made a weak and unproven attempt at defining my core purpose in life, but seriously, how was I to know? How is one to know? How do we just pull something like purpose or destiny out and define it on the spot because we're asked to? It was far easier to focus mainly on a long set of goals and habits.

What else do you want to do?

What do you want to be?

What skills do you want to have?

Out poured an inventory of industries and areas I wished to be a part of over the course of my life and a series of other seemingly unrelated objectives. The list was long and entirely unreasonable. At the very top: '#1 Visit space'. Then a pocketful of goals, ideas and things I wanted to do exploded onto the page: '#3 Write a children's book; #20 Build a global consumer brand; #16 Learn the piano; #17 Master Mandarin; #12 Create a fashion label; #9 Own a bar; #25 Develop a chain of premium hotels; #28 Learn to ride a horse; #34 Work with Richard Branson.'

I didn't stop to think about the hows or the whys; I just pressed ink every time I thought of something. Napoleon kept pushing me on through the pages. 'Now, you need to tell me — what kind of personality traits do you want to home in on? What are some of the things you really need to improve on — everybody can improve, in any area of their life. What do you want to be better at?'

Back then if I had a bad day, I could easily get a bit down and turn a single sharp blow into a session of hard drinks at night, so I wrote, 'Positivity: Only allow positive thoughts to occupy my mind.' Because I sometimes shied away from signing up to things I didn't know how to do well, or approaching people in social settings that I should go up and say hello to, I wrote, 'Courage: Carry out forced acts of small courage repeatedly.' Because I knew that I was sometimes too blunt and spoke my thoughts at the exact moment they streamed into my head, I wrote, 'I will be less brutally honest. Think before speaking.'

In the most unusual request, Mr Hill moved into the territory of creating an imaginary circle of relationships. 'Create a council of the people of today and in history, to inspire you.

Who would be on it and what would you want from them? List their names and from here on out, imagine them helping you through all your decisions.'

By the time I'd done with that I had exactly 60 people across five categories, handpicked as channels of inspiration. There were military and political leaders of history, Alexander the Great, Napoleon, Churchill, the Kennedys and Gandhi; artists, writers and poets, Picasso, Tennyson and Hemingway; entrepreneurs, entertainers, visionaries and industrialists, Walt Disney, Frank Sinatra and Andrew Carnegie. The list traversed all centuries and all parts of the planet.

'How much money do you want to have, by when and for what? Write it down! Commit it to paper.'

I thought about this for a few days, and started with $10 million. Ten million seemed like a reasonable amount. A few days passed. I scratched it out and wrote $100 million. A few more days passed and I just couldn't see the difference in aiming for $100 million over a billion — they both seemed ridiculous, but I figured if there are people in the world who are going to end up as billionaires, and I've got a lifetime ahead, one of them might as well be me. Even if I end up with 1 per cent of that it wouldn't be all that bad. No point aiming low, so I committed to paper, 'I will have a net worth of US$1bn by 2018 (age 40).'

This went on for weeks. Hill would ask the questions and I'd try to answer them. There were just *too* many but I tried anyway and waded through them one by one until he was wearing me down.

'What are you going to give for it?

'You have to give.

'You have to work — things don't come for nothing.

'What are you going to sacrifice for what you want?' Napoleon pushed.

To be honest, I really didn't understand the question.

'What do you *think* I'm going to give? Well I'm going to work my ass off. I can work. I know how to grind out the hours, day after day, week after week. I know that things don't come easy. I'll do whatever it takes to build businesses that get me to my goals. I'll put in the effort and work and learn and try and work and work and work, until I get what I want. What else could you possibly mean other than that?'

By the end of that summer I had started what I would eventually turn into a part of my DNA — forced, quiet periods of reflection that I began to call my *white space*. Here I was, returning home with my Moleskine under my arm. In it, I had my first real plan. I had my first real inventory of goals, my first real cut at a silhouette of somebody I thought I wanted to be. I had started to design a vision of my life; a picture was being painted, stroke by stroke, branching across everything I thought I loved and wanted, across all genres, places, people and fortunes, a picture of a holistic group of adventures wrapped into a single interwoven vehicle to make them happen. I visualised a brand and image of a collection of enterprises within 10 years, integrating all the areas I loved in life so that I could love them in work as well. I had seen and heard about these amazing people from afar — people who built up a portfolio of interests and assets across a myriad of life's passions; people who looked like they had it all. That is what I wanted to be.

It was of course a pipe dream but at least it was a dream, and I figured *some* of it would come true, right?

I felt like this roller coaster I had been sitting in through this whole trip around the world, clicking and creaking higher

Shoot for the moon — even if you miss you'll land among the stars.

and higher with every new discovery and decision, had finally made it to the top and when it got there, it paused. I was suspended from time and space, ready to be unleashed and swoop back into the world. I made my way back to New Zealand, all of a sudden in a desperate hurry with an urge to quickly make a start on it all before time ran out. As flawed as it might have been, from my few weeks away, each of the pieces I *thought* I needed to have in my picture, every possible piece that I thought might make me a happy, successful person, made it into a list. The what, the who, the how and the where was all mapped out with every piece ready and willing, just waiting for me to meet it.

Every single piece except one.

Turning Ideas Into Action:

THE FIELD

GUIDE

Everybody has ideas. Everybody wants to do things. Nobody 'has the time'. This section is a practical guide to uncovering what is most meaningful and important to you — and starting.

ACTING AS IF

**'Whether you think you can
or you can't, you're right.'**

Henry Ford

Your mindset, how you perceive the world to be and your role in it, ultimately has a greater impact on how the story of your life plays out than anything. More than talent, breeding, education, luck, circumstances, strength – more than anything. Self-belief and your mental attitude unlock the keys to life.

Influencing the subconscious until it believes itself is a technique as old as the gods. For good or for bad, belief is the dictator of the mind: whatever you believe in, you become.

You need to start believing as soon as you feel able to; the paradox is that you can begin *before* you start something, or *as* you start something. Often you just need to start (even if you don't believe you can finish) and that very act spurs on belief.

After that initial leap, blind faith alone is not much use – it may work in religion but not in life. Equally, the brash confidence of unfounded talent does more damage than drive results. Posting and espousing reams of inspirational quotes and expecting 'karma' to do all the work without turning the mantras into *real* action in your own life is equally hopeless. Unless you build practical strengths in what you are trying to achieve, then there is no practical use believing in it.

Belief *must* be backed by strength, dedication and commitment. If you believe you can go to the moon, you need to know that you can find the strength and resources to execute a plan to achieve the goal. Believe. Plan. Strengthen. Execute.

The more you take those initial leaps of faith, the more you are able to look back and say, 'Hey, I tried that, and I *did* it' and the deeper your wells of confidence become; wells that you can draw upon when you need them for the next leap. The more leaps you take and the harder you work to back up that faith, the more you can genuinely believe in the faith you are putting in yourself. Ultimately, you reach a point where

Sometimes, our minds need to be tricked into believing; the doing and being just has to catch up with the believing.

there is just a *knowing* that this is going to happen and that you are capable of making it happen. Here are just a few of the ways to help you get there:

- Talking to yourself
- Building or breaking habits
- Visualisation
- Inspiration

TALKING TO YOURSELF

The first cynic you have to silence is yourself. Your own mind talks to itself — this is not a sign of insanity, it's the reality of every single daily interaction and action you make. The only problem is that it often tells you that you *can't* do something. Any action you take is either subconscious or conscious. The subconscious is a place that has been trained for so long that thoughts and actions become natural and on autopilot. Until you train your mind to move something into the subconscious, everything is active in your conscious and that's where it stays.

If you tell yourself something often enough, you will soon believe it. There are two sharp sides to that blade, and it cuts both ways, for positive *and* negative thoughts. For good or for bad, we are what we think.

Even in situations where something is not

quite a reality or I don't quite yet have what I need, I can speak and act *as if I do*. The more you talk yourself into something, the more it becomes 'not an option' to fail.

In the early days of our journey, we started to use the term 'liestones', a dyslexic redesign of 'milestones', to indicate what we needed to achieve in our future and to behave as if they were already achieved. A lie is a false statement with the deliberate intent to deceive – agreed. However, when you tell a liestone, you are trying to deceive *your own mind*, your own confidence.

We would talk about technical challenges with no clear solution in sight as if they had already been met; we would tell ourselves that we had a headcount of 10 when we only had seven – in our mind the other three were just people we were waiting to find; to feel the gravity of the next revenue milestone we'd say, 'We are a million-dollar company', when our turnover was, say, $650,000, because we fully believed we were on track to be one and it was just a matter of time. Sometimes, our minds need to be *tricked* into believing; the doing and being just has to catch up with the believing.

BUILDING OR BREAKING HABITS

Whatever you focus on starts to become a reality, so if you believe you are not good at something or not capable of it, then there is virtually no chance of you ever being able to do it well. If you are the type of person who defends yourself as 'not good at remembering people's names' or 'always late', then sure enough, you will *never* be good at remembering people's names and you will *always* be late simply because you've already talked your way into it. If you change your strategy by just a few degrees and think, 'I am not good at remembering people's names *right now*, but I am going to become great at it', this will soon change. Of course, saying it is not enough – if you did a little research, created a plan to build or acquire strength and then started executing it in small ways, you'll be on your way. A little Google work, and 15 minutes at your desk sketching a few new habits to form, and the next time you are at a party you will in no time be challenging yourself to make it happen.

Learning new things and breaking old habits is nothing more than building or immersing yourself in new ones, then having the mental stamina to *stick* to them until they are formed.

The methods to become good at practically *anything* are well known to humanity and often freely available on the internet. You just have to find them, develop a personal style to train yourself, commit to them *mentally* – and habitually invest in building strengths or breaking weaknesses. If you are late, start designing and building habits to gradually be early; if you talk too much and don't listen enough, gradually build a plan to start hearing what people say more and holding your tongue; if you seem to have the same ideas as everybody else, gradually create the habit of pushing yourself for five, 10, 20 minutes a day to come up with ideas that are genuinely unique to the world (or at least your part of it).

Start small.

VISUALISATION

Visualising what it is you wish for yourself is one of the most powerful tools I know and it's free to anybody who has a functioning imagination. Moving beyond imagination to existence, there's a good reason why creating a brand identity or short video describing an idea starts to move it towards reality – it brings it to life. It energises it visually, through sound, motion and graphics, and makes it feel real. Often when you're starting a new project, company, play, book or whatever it is, the moment you visualise what it might *look* or sound like, the moment you agree on, say, the name, it begins to feel like something is happening. With that feeling comes momentum, motivation and inspiration to push ahead.

Genius is the ability to put into effect what is on your mind.

F. Scott Fitzgerald

Kickstarter.com is the leading 'crowd funding' service that enables personal dreams to come true through the funding of micro amounts from the general public in response purely to a stranger pitching an idea. It's those video pitches that the entrepreneurs, artists and activists seeking funding have to perfect to make their story seem believable and on the verge of happening if only the crowd would help fund it into existence. They are brilliant examples of what happens when you visualise a concept into something more tangible – the mere act of doing that moves it off the drawing board and into motion.

In his extraordinary book *The Winner's Bible*, neuroscientist Kerry Spackman emphasises the importance of 'rewiring your brain for permanent change' and strongly advocates representing the dreams and goals you have as visually as possible. He goes as far as suggesting we all create a visual diary solely for that purpose and also talks about creating potent audio recordings for the elite athletes and professionals he works with to listen to, to overcome mental blocks.

I have a coach, Karen Hamilton, who helps me plan and achieve my highest priorities. We have used her version of this type of approach to get me comfortable in advance of major moments: we sit and I close my eyes with my feet grounded on the floor as we talk through the feeling of executing what it is I need to do. We extend this further and meditate on how it feels when it's done, describing in detail the surroundings and emotions and the effects on myself and the people around me that result from the achievement of this meeting, discussion or turning point. It gives me a very solid footing to do battle with my thoughts, playing out the reactions or rejections of others before I enter the arena.

I use a combination of tools and methods and continue to develop them, totally convinced of the power of autosuggestion, and visualising yourself in a situation. This applies equally to both the big and small things in life.

You need to create something that works for you. Some of the ideas above might sound silly, but it's not a coincidence that the greatest achievers in sport, art and life have all adopted some formula of instilling and nurturing self-belief. Perhaps at times, nobody else believed in them, so they had to create their own situations where they believed so strongly in themselves that they convinced others too. In the world of global sports today there is no greater example of this idea than the rise of Andy Murray: his tennis isn't any better than it was when he couldn't help but lose under pressure, but his mind has dramatically improved. This is thanks to his new coach, Ivan Lendl, who has also lived the repeated failures that Murray was living through and has clearly devised and shared his mental strategies to overcome them.

We are what we repeatedly do.

Aristotle

INSPIRATION

Finally, inspiration is an enormous source of self-belief. For most of my life I have invested a considerable proportion of my time building layer upon layer of self-belief through the achievements and stories of *others*. I have studied, read and observed their lives and their amazing feats to convince myself that if they can do *that*, I can do *this*. This simple premise underpins much of my own self-belief and is rooted in fact: the fact that another human being has achieved feats of an extraordinary nature with no greater superpowers than the powers we have each been gifted with at birth. Inspiration plays a role not only in motivating you, but in giving you the belief that we are capable of anything we put our minds to.

Inspiration through the lives of others comes packaged in many forms: in movies and music; books and biographies; magazines and images; speeches, interviews or the news. It may come from actors, adventurers or activists. Inspiration can even come through imaginary characters in imaginary stories in imaginary worlds.

STARTING

How can anything be more important than starting if all that you do before is simply in preparation for the day you begin? The moment you decide to start is very often when things decide to start happening.

Starting with small actions towards an ambitious aspiration is a very good way to begin. A key thing that keeps me grounded yet bold is running parallel paths – the development of a compelling vision at the same time as the creation of a finite action plan of to-do's.

Many people become obsessed with their 'great idea'. The world is not short of great ideas; they happen every second in every corner of the planet and are rarely unique or genuinely new. More often than not it is the *execution* that wins. Steve Jobs didn't invent the mouse (Xerox did); he didn't invent digital music players (Kane Kramer did); he wasn't the first to have the idea that the phone was a device for connectivity and media (many others had this revelation long before). What made Apple what it was in the decade to 2010 was its execution – in totally original ways – often by piecing together concepts and understandings that already existed into something that, when combined, was unparalleled and *appeared* entirely new.

Holding on tightly to ideas these days is outdated. Despite that, being committed to an idea *before* you've had a chance to allow it to breathe and to compete with others in your mind is a rash risk that people trying to launch projects often take. That's why it's important to have a personal 'start filter' to help you think through and select what ideas ultimately earn the privilege of getting out of the gates.

YOUR START FILTER

Sometimes it works: you rush off to the races, your gut was right and you end up creating something incredible that you and everybody loves. But far more often it doesn't: you shot out the gates with a half-baked idea that probably wasn't great in the first place, and worse than that, as you are developing it you come up with dozens of better ones that compete with it in your mind.

Determining the shortlist of all the possible things you could do are decisions that relate to your personal vision of your life, the purpose you wish to fulfil and the major milestones you have set for yourself in the coming one, three, five or even 10 years. Many people have a 'bucket list' of all the things they think they want to do — that's a decent place to start. If you *haven't* created such a sketch of what you think your life should look like in the future — even if it's just scribbled down on a scrap of paper or a napkin — then you'd better start. A life without even the simplest map is the ultimate testament to the saying, 'if you don't know where you're going, any road will get you there'.

Wherever you are now and however you see yourself today can have as much or as little relevance as you choose to where you want to be or who you want to become in the future. If you are so deep down a track that you feel, though you're in fact only half committed, you've gone too far in to switch careers or plans, think again. It's never too late to purposefully *design* the life you always dreamed of living, and bit by bit go about making it happen.

Life is short. We don't have time to invest in average ideas. That's why your start filter is critical: what idea gets the privilege of accessing your time, energy and resources and gets to the starting blocks? In energy management, just as in time management, the filter that only you can control is what will maximise your return on energy and emotional commitment in whatever endeavours you embark on — from learning a new skill to starting a new business. Some of the things to consider from a commitment and personal perspective include:

- Alignment with your core values. Does this project align with all your core values or do you have alternative motives?
- If there are alternative motives, what are they? Money, fame, boredom? You want to be sure that you do things based on drivers that will last the test of time. Is this idea just a reaction to a temporary feeling that might fade in a few months or years?
- The time commitment required. Is this going to be 'all in' or a part-time commitment? If it's a part-time commitment, exactly how much of your time are you committing and exactly when will you schedule that time to ensure you can deliver? How much time can you commit now? What do you need to stop doing to free up enough time to work on this? Is this something you are committing to for a month, a year or more? If you are going all in, how will you phase in from whatever you are doing now?
- The risk of failure and your tolerance for risk *today*. How much risk can you take? With any new adventure you may be risking time, energy, emotion, reputation and sometimes money. What is your tole-rance right now? Are you comfortable

financially and socially? Do you feel confident to take a big leap and be able to bounce back, or are you just coming off the back of a series of defeats and need a breather?

- The scale of the vision and pay-off. Are you looking to make a dent in the universe or just notch up a small win? Are you swinging for the fences or trying to tackle some low-hanging fruit? Setting the right height for your goals first will determine how you assess opportunities that come your way.

PUBLICISING OR PRIVATISING?

Do you share your idea, putting it out there publicly that you are embarking on something and risk the entire world knowing about it and *stealing* it from you? Or do you keep it close to your chest and guard it fiercely? Some possible benefits of going public with an idea, even to a small group of friends at first, include:

- Public 'beta'. In software there is an expression that an idea is 'in beta' before it is properly launched to the world. During this phase users are invited to participate, knowing that the product has flaws and the level of service will be lower; however, they are also invited to help shape the product. In sharing ideas, you can adopt a similar approach with a small group of trusted people – or even openly through digital media – and clearly state that you are just 'putting it out there' to see what people think. In this way you aren't committing to execution, you are committed to exploration.

- Feedback signals. Once you share an idea or a plan, people can't help but add to it, build it, critique it, question it or dismiss it. If you are paying close attention and ensuring that you don't have myopia over your own idea, every single piece of feedback and signal you pick up can help you shape your idea for the better.

- Accountability. If you've moved beyond exploration and you've said that you're going to do it, if you have any integrity whatsoever, then you'd better go and do it. At the very minimum you need to take action and put in a very good effort. This is very encouraging and a form of positive peer pressure, and I use it selectively for certain things. It *forces* me to do something because I've put my reputation out there by telling people I really respect that I will do it.

- Early abandonment. Sharing an idea may

ultimately even lead to you abandoning it altogether, having been convinced through all the data points and feedback that it isn't as strong as you first thought. In many cases, considered and decisive early abandonment of something you were about to dedicate enormous amounts of energy to is a much less painful decision than pulling the plug after having committed and begun.

Some of the disadvantages of going public with an idea include:

- Being *too* malleable. Prematurely sharing something before you've properly thought it through creates the risk that if you haven't looked at all the supporting insights, angles, possibilities and downfalls, the concept may appear amorphous and weak. In this state it can easily be subject to disproportionate influence from everyone you speak to, and you might find yourself constantly reshaping it based on the ideas and feedback the *most recent* person gave you. To avoid this you have to have a firm place to stand with a robust case, but be flexible to change.
- Public retractions. If in the process of sharing you learn that this is something

Murder your darlings.

Arthur Quiller-Couch

you think you are better off discontinuing, then you must smartly and honourably face up to its closure and communicate why you have chosen to abandon course. People will admire your courage for making a difficult decision and informing them properly, even though it may make you look fickle. However, if this becomes a pattern, you will gain a reputation as a 'starter' who can't complete things. We all know people like this — they describe themselves as 'an ideas person, a creative big picture thinker' and they start half-baked ventures, books, new courses, sports, ideas or endeavours constantly with none of them ever getting to fruition. You *don't* want to be this person — you want to be the person who has really thought something through and is committed to their bold ideas. You want to be the person people can *trust* to follow through.

HABITS AND FOCUS

Whatever it is you do in life, you are built on the habits that shape your behaviour. Habits make the man. Habits make the woman. When you think of the word 'habit', initially you may think of bad habits such as being late or talking over somebody when they are speaking. But really what you should be focused on mentally are good habits and the habits you *want* to have. Expand your understanding of what a habit is to include, say, your tone of voice, your ability to focus relentlessly in a world with ever-increasing distractions, or a habit to ensure you do the important over the urgent.

THE COVEY QUADRANT

The late Stephen Covey was a giant in the world of productivity and focus. He wrote the book *The 7 Habits of Highly Effective People* as the result of interviewing hundreds of successful people to find out how they got so much done. A handful of the tools he developed are a fundamental part of my productivity arsenal today – the first and most important is the Covey Quadrant, laid out below. The horizontal axis is the level of urgency; the vertical axis is the level of importance; and they intersect to create four quadrants.

The simple underlying idea behind this quadrant is that the vast majority of people in their working and personal lives *prioritise the urgent* far more highly than the *important*. Re-read that sentence again and then, thinking about the last week, review the things you put at the top of your list that needed getting done: were they urgent, time-sensitive tasks? Or were they ensuring you spent two hours in solitude working on your life plan and goals, refining your values or investing in reviewing what you had learned the week before to set improvements you might make for the future? The former are Quadrant 1 (Q1) tasks, the latter are Q2 investments. The former are *noise*: urgency, ticking of boxes and a hive of action in the present; the latter are *signal*: thoughtful, meaningful progress to create the future.

Q3 is just filled with what life is too short to be doing, and Q4 is the killer of society's productivity, compounded by the internet, Facebook, Twitter and the socialisation of the web sucking 230,060 years out of Americans in one month in 2012 alone.

URGENT

NOT URGENT

IMPORTANT

I
- Crises
- Pressing problems
- Deadline-driven stuff
- Last minute prep & chaos

II
- Preparation
- Values clarification
- Planning & thinking
- Relationships
- Risk Mgmt

NOT IMPORTANT

III
- Interruptions — some phone calls
- Some mail, reports
- Some meetings
- A lot of popular activities
- Other people's minor issues

IV
- Time wasting — a lot of web browsing, facebook ++
- Most TV
- "Busywork"
- Trivia — useless info.

Technology and social norms have stolen time and productivity from us and replaced them with tools of distraction – we have to fight our hardest to get our time back on our own terms.

If you are somebody who finds yourself constantly in Q1 (putting out fires, staying up late because you have a deadline tomorrow, always frenzied picking things up, dropping things off and always ending the day with more on your to-do list than when you started), it's most likely because you are not spending anywhere near enough time in Q2. But how can you afford to spend *any* time at all on the things that aren't urgent, when you have *all* these urgent things to attend to? You don't have the time to be planning, preparing, thinking of possible scenarios or sitting there thinking about your future for hours, right?

The correct answer is: you can't afford *not* to. How do I know? By observing the hundreds of people I have hired and worked with and got to know in my personal life – those who always appear excessively busy and hectic, have no order, no sense of planning or priorities, and react to whatever is calling them the loudest; they thrive on the chaos but often don't get anything important done. They could live and die in Q1 achieving nothing meaningful in life if they're not careful. There is no meaning living in Q1. Meaning is found in Q2; that is the one and only quadrant where meaning and true success

Never confuse action with progress.

is found, so a fundamental goal of life is to spend as little time in Q1 and spend *as much time as possible* in Q2.

If we know it's critical to invest in the important, *why* is it so easy to default to the urgent? The urgent appears in small, bite-sized tasks – emails, phone calls and situations you may recognise by the following statements: 'I'll just quickly...', 'I just need to send this off...', 'I just need to finish this...', 'I'll just be five minutes...'

If you don't address the *important*, and instead chase the urgent for weeks, months (or in some cases I've seen, *years*) – you are chasing things not worth chasing. You are removing meaning from your life, and ultimately diminishing your impact. The way time flies, you can easily be sitting in the same job five years after you started, and looking back realise that all you see is a series of urgencies linked together in one long chain of meaninglessness.

As counter-intuitive as this sounds, the *more* time you steal from your 'urgent' tasks at hand, to spend in Q2, the fewer urgent tasks you will end up having to deal with. So how do you start?

Here are some practical tips:

- When you write a list of things, spend the time to review the root cause of why something becomes urgent and what could have been done earlier to create a solution that would reduce the frequency of this task becoming urgent in the future. Then, immediately schedule and protect some time to work on the solution to remove the *source* of the urgent.

- Review your week ahead, and carve out some time to focus *only* on the things that are not due for at least 100 days or have no timeline to them at all. Important things. Protect this time with your life and, whatever happens, make 100 per cent sure that you commit to it – use it to work on yourself and your goals. If you are so busy that you can't start with an hour, then start with just 15 minutes and slowly increase it each week.
- If you can master the Covey Quadrant, you can master your time. If you can master your time, you can master your energy. After 10 years of believing in it, I still at times find myself stuck in Q1, so once you've started it's something you have to keep reminding yourself and refreshing – build time in the week *just* to do that.
- And in what follows: Rocks and Pebbles, Going Analogue, and From Lists to Action.

ROCKS AND PEBBLES

Rocks are things that really matter. They are the *strategic* actions or *milestones* that get you closer to your biggest dreams and goals. At any point in time, there should be very few of them – if there were many, they wouldn't be strategic or milestones.

Each week, determine what the rocks for the week will be – I try to never have more than three to five personally, and a similar number for a small team.

Each day, pick one or two *mandatories* that are rocks for that day. These are the things that absolutely must get done today, will contribute to the weekly rocks, and if you achieve them you will feel meaningful satisfaction. They must also qualify as being something that pushes you visibly towards your major strategic goals of the week or month – they move the needle. Like many things in life, there's an 80/20 rule – 80 per cent of the things you think you need to do are pebbles and don't move the needle; 20 per cent (or less) are rocks and move mountains.

You can keep working outwards from here – what are the three rocks for the month? The five rocks for this calendar quarter? The 10 rocks for the year? Working backwards from the main things you want to achieve in a distinct period into smaller and smaller chunks of time ensures that you are always focusing on things that are going to move you forward to your *longer-term* goals.

Often you can recognise rocks because they have inertia – they are mentally hard to start. Here is the single most important rule to roll your rocks over: *do them first*. The day doesn't start until they get done – no phone calls, no emails, no surfing, no meetings. The longer you wait in the day until you hit these core tasks, the more distractions will pop up, and the noise of the day increases to the point where you lose the opportunity for total clarity. Before you know it the day is over.

GOING ANALOGUE AND OFFLINE

People often ask me in a world of constant connectivity how I can just ignore all communication channels for two, three or four hours in the morning – and some days or weeks, entirely – and the answer is simple: I know that if I *don't*, I will be stuck in the same trap as everybody else and start fighting the sparks of urgency, leaving the 'important' burning away slowly in the background waiting for me to attend to it.

Some people create entirely separate physical spaces to think in analogue – a traditional desk, with pens, markers, notepads and sketchbooks. Working manually, with 'hand tools' to create plans and ideas, seems to draw out a very different type of thinking than what we generate when attached to a mouse and keyboard. Having a tactile canvas and instruments to work through complex ideas and thoughts can be a much more visceral experience than constantly relying on the digital.

FROM LISTS TO ACTION

When you start your day, try NOT to connect to anything. This is the easiest trap to fall into that turns the morning (and then the day) into a spiral that gets out of *your* control. Do not connect your laptop or phone – stay *offline* until you have made significant progress on the rocks of the day. How?

- Turn your phone to airplane (offline) mode.
- Turn your wifi off. If you're on an ethernet connection, pull the plug out.
- If you think you need to use the internet to get your rocks done, then use a site blocker to block Facebook, Twitter and all the sites that can eat up your time.
- You can still write and access emails in your mail program while you are offline. You could also just use Notepad or a knowledge-filing application like Evernote to write any critical emails you

need to write and then copy and paste
them when you get back online.

- Do not check email as the first task of
the day. For many people, email is the
worst productivity tool ever invented.
Take control of your inbox. We all know
how it feels to have lost hours refreshing
our inbox and reacting to emails here
and there with no strategic impact to
our day and our goals — be goal-led, not
response-driven.

- Never multi-task. Multi-tasking is a myth
of our generation. It never works. Our
minds can only focus on one thing *well*.
This means never browsing the internet
while on a conference call or talking
during writing.

- Write shorter lists. Try and aim to get
less done each day. Set yourself up to
succeed so that you can feel like you're
getting ahead.

- Schedule *clear time* in your calendar; time
that isn't scheduled for anything but is
protected. You'll be thankful when it arrives
each day and you get to it. You will either
be behind on your core tasks and need the
clear time to catch up or you can use it
for your pebbles. If nothing else, you can
spend it on some strategic planning.

- Write 'to don't' lists. Write a list of the
things you *won't do*, because knowing those

things is just as impactful as knowing what you *will* do.

- Time and place 'shift'. Use online tools to minimise your distractions by moving something from the here and now to the there and later. For example, if you are online and looking for something specific but stumble across an article, you do not need to read it *immediately* or keep it open in a tab in your browser. It's OK to postpone when it's read and where you read it. Install and use the Instapaper bookmark to save the article to read it later when it won't distract you, or on your mobile phone while waiting for a coffee or somebody to arrive. You can use similar tools like Watchlater to do the same thing for videos that you see in your Facebook or Twitter feed that you shouldn't watch right now, or long TED videos that you don't have the time to concentrate on this very minute. With these tools you tag the videos and queue them for future watching at a better time to avoid getting sidetracked. In the end I've found for most of the articles and videos, even though I know I can go back to them, I never do. This underscores how they weren't really that important in the first place – this goes for probably 95 per cent of the content you consume online.

Besides the noble art of getting things done, there is the noble art of leaving things undone. The wisdom of life consists in the elimination of non-essentials.

Lin Yutang

- Use the Action Method to 'file' everything. Scott Belsky wrote a book called *The Action Method*, in which he suggests that for every item that comes across your day you file it into one of only three buckets: action, reference or backburner. I use Evernote to store reference and backburner items, and tag them as such under different folders representing projects or contexts. I use a web-app task management tool like Luumin to store, edit and then print out the short-term task list that I check off as I go, all synced on my phone.

Time is invaluable. How we spend it is how we spend our lives. Wasting our time is wasting our lives.

BEING CONNECTED

To live a big, impactful life, we all could do well to think of ourselves as citizens of the world – *and act that way*. A big part of this is constantly being in touch with our global surroundings. With the internet and social media, being permanently *digitally* connected is easy; but, being genuinely *personally* connected seems to be getting harder and harder – while being entirely *disconnected* at times to free up the space needed to extract personal meaning from this myriad of constant connections and information is the hardest but most important thing to be able to do.

Here are five ways to stay globally connected:

Create your kaleidoscope

Curate your sources of viewpoints, news and culture. Develop a portfolio of websites, books, communities, bars, interests or television shows that collectively represent a well-balanced *global* perspective on the world — especially in subjects and areas that you don't typically love or engage with. Stimulus from outside what we are used to being stimulated by is often what stretches our minds the most. I try to expose myself to the greatest, most inspiring achievements and ideas that people have ever created or know — and to integrate them into my life so they shape my expectations of the world.

All of these sources serve to puncture the daily cycles of what our minds easily process, and prod us with questions and ideas we are less often exposed to. The more difficult it is for our mind to process or understand something that is new or uncommon, the more of a workout we're giving it. Make an effort to try to surround yourself with people from different parts of the planet, and from different walks of life. Expose yourself to and explore their cultures and ideologies. There is always something to learn within them and they give you an invaluable worldwide mirror on everything you think and say. Many people lean on too-localised sources for their inspiration and sometimes get trapped in a bubble of not only local content but hyper-local networks where they lose touch with their greater surroundings and the world at large.

Benchmark globally

One prominent by-product of thinking outwards and internationally versus insularly and locally is that your comparative set changes. Instead of worrying about what they're doing up the road, you start thinking about what they're doing in Shanghai, or London, or San Francisco. At The Hyperfactory our ambition was always to be considered among the very best in the world at what we did. We knew that putting everything else aside, if we achieved this status then all other things should fall into place. Every step of the way we benchmarked ourselves against the global forerunners, global trends and global breakthroughs. We wanted our name mentioned in their company – we wanted our name headlining their company.

Zoom out

Change your scale; whatever is your passion or whatever drives you most, take the time to step away from it and consider the bigger questions of the world. Consider the moon, the planets and stars light years away, the health that you have and the war and poverty that others stuggle in. Stay in touch with those who are trying to advance humanity on the biggest scale and you will always provide yourself humility and context for what matters and what doesn't (watching TED videos is a good exercise for that). Use this to balance your attention towards both ends of the spectrum of what changes the world and what changes *your* world.

Get on planes

Travel for exploration — as often as you can. Travelling constantly for work makes it routine to book a trip, pack a suitcase and get on a plane for a job, but when you get home the last thing you might want to do is get on *another* flight — I know this as much as anyone might. Even so, I also know how important it is to be immersed in another culture for the purpose of your *own development* rather than purely the development of a business plan or for a getaway.

Once it becomes seamless to you to get on a plane the distances contract and your mind expands. Yes, your wallet is poorer, but your life is far richer, and with websites like AirBnB that enable you to find inexpensive places to stay in other people's homes, there are many ways to make global travel affordable.

For many people, travelling is where you get your ideas. You see the world in a different way, which ends up in you seeing things differently when you come back home.

Avoid flytraps of myopia

Communities that gravitate obsessively around myopic perspectives and over-associate with their own kind start falling into their own language and subculture (unintelligible to the outside) complete with a belief that their world might be more important than the rest of whatever the planet may be doing. This is a common jargon and acronym-filled theme with the technology and venture capital start-up world, which panders to websites like TechCrunch.com as the overlord of everything. This is replicated in another world I have spent a lot of time in: advertising and marketing. In certain advertising agencies you will find circles of people who may think that the work they are doing is the most important in the world, on par with the great moviemakers and artists of history. It might have something to do with the ego trip of seeing your work on national television or with the association of the money that the people in charge control. (Of course it's not their money, but everybody that wants to secure some of it treats them as if it is.)

I still love those industries, don't get me wrong — but I am more careful now than ever not to get consumed by them; there is a lot to love about technology start-ups, and there is still a little bit to love about advertising!

Whatever community you identify with most,

don't let it define you. Don't get so carried away in your own circle of awesomeness that you drown out the amazing things you can learn and experience by being open to, *listening* to and connecting with multiple circles of apparently unrelated networks and interests. Strive to be multi-dimensional and you will probably lead a far more interesting life.

CONNECTED TEAMS

To do anything meaningful and scalable you need a team. For some people this is obvious, such as President Obama with an entire administration behind him, or a rugby star like All Black Richie McCaw with 14 players beside him. But even individual heroes, who appear on the surface to do it all alone, have a team. Usain Bolt has a team. Serena Williams has a team. Michael Schumacher had a team. Behind what on the face of it is individual success, there is almost always *a complete team*. Teams win championships, not players; instead of obsessing with fixing individual weaknesses, teams focus on building strengths, to compensate and balance towards building a whole body and brain that is infinitely better and more synchronised than the sum of its parts.

People behave differently under different conditions, so you need to be aware of the

None of us is as smart as all of us.

Sir Ray Avery

nuances of people's stronger and weaker sides. Stress creates a 'shadow' side; people default to this mode under pressure and it is possible to get an idea what this might look like in advance of you having to witness it first-hand. If you are interested in testing your default conditions under stress, there are assessment methodologies that allow you to visualise this kind of information and learn a little more about yourself.

One such tool is called the 'Whole Brain Thinking Styles' assessment and was created by Ned Herrmann at his consultancy Herrmann International. I actively use it to preview people who I might work with, and to manage my self-awareness of my natural strengths and weaknesses. It is an assessment that identifies your preferred thinking approach to help you understand whether you are really more emotional, analytical, structural or strategic in how you process situations and information. The overall premise of using the 'whole brain' thesis when forming a team of connections is that instead of just piecing together experience and skill sets, you are concentrating on the behavioural attributes and *preferred thinking styles* of each of the team members in order to create a holistic, balanced brain.

It takes depths of courage to ask all the hard questions of yourself and of others; to really look inside; to *think*; to critique and challenge your *own* assumptions. We are burdened by our own subconscious and our own histories – 'experience' guides us and shadows views and paths that we might otherwise have strongly considered. That is precisely why we need to create connected and holistic teams that challenge each other as much as they support each other.

GIVE

You don't just wake up one morning and get connected. The most valuable technique for building a strong network of impactful relationships I can ever give anybody is the following: whatever you think you have, or are good at, or can offer, *give some of it away freely and often*. People just *do not expect* you to offer something for nothing. The world doesn't work like that any more, so if you are the one who is working that way, you stand out like a beacon of hope for humanity and kindness.

Something has been lost in the world when it comes to the giving of talent, time and treasure with very little expectation in return. I can *guarantee* you the more you give to people, the more the world will give back to you. I'm *not* talking money or things that are easy to give like a can of soup (although that can be important too). I'm talking about your energy, your passion, your brains, reputation and perhaps most importantly and valuably: your time.

It won't be a consistently predictable equation (if you give y, you get x in return), but in the long run, I have never had this formula fail on me. Something very interesting happens when you start to give: *you* are in control. Because you are offering something that is not bound by an expectation or a 'contract', you are the one in charge of the resources because you have proffered them with no strings attached. If for some reason you are unhappy with what you've got yourself into, you can simply walk away and you owe nothing to anybody. We do get sick of people who are always wanting or asking for something without opening up a two-way street. Everyday I get an email from a stranger asking me for my time, money, ideas or feedback – 99 per cent of them have never stopped to think of even the tiniest thing they might be able to offer or help me with. The people who stand out in our minds as those we want to be around are those who do the most to help other people without being asked to – they are constantly offering up time, advice, ideas, thoughts or connections to help you advance your cause instead of just pushing their own. This is one of the most basic truisms of life, yet apparently one of the hardest to follow.

AMBITION
TO ACTION

A lot of people struggle with successfully juggling many things at the same time. People struggle to turn personal ideas or desires into action. Outside of the weight of a daily routine people really do find it hard to break through the mental inertia to balance the long-term dreams with the short-term realities — in short, a lot of people struggle to go from *heart to start*.

It's perfectly OK to admit this — none of us are superhuman and because dreams are free, and time is short, none of us could get everything we ever wanted to do done, which is why it's so important to force yourself to prioritise, to name the things you *won't* do, and to make sure the things you *will* do are the ones that will most serve your personal purpose in life. After all of this the most important thing of all is just to *start*. Over the last decade I've synthesised the best of the best of people who have created popular systems that work well for some and work less well for others. I've mentioned Scott Belsky, whose brilliant book *The Action Method* is tailored to people in the creative industries; Stephen Covey, whose various books (including *The 7 Habits of Highly Effective People*) and training programmes (including *Focus*) have covered so much ground for all types of people to start developing a personal action and development regime; business author Jim Collins has been repeatedly quoted about 'white space', a concept that I have also referred to in this book – the sacred *scheduled and protected* time where there is nothing booked other than to think, read, plan and be creative or strategic.

There are many more ideas and frameworks designed to enable you to lead a more impactful life. I have found that none of them worked for me by themselves – because nobody is the same; you need to pick and choose the bits that work for you. I've spent years fine-tuning a personal synthesis of a system and structure that suits *my* idiosyncrasies and needs. It's a continuous work in progress. Below I've shared the overarching skeleton of how it works. Many people will be allergic to what appears to be such rigidity; however, what looks like inflexible structure in fact is a regime that provides *freedom within a framework*. It's being grounded in that structure itself that is precisely what gives me the flexibility to be creative, spontaneous and instinctive within it.

The framework breaks my year into discrete chunks of time to plan – looking out various distances into the future – the 1000, 100, 30, 10 and one-day periods.

The 1000

Once a year, a longer-range three-to-five-year and mid-range one-year planning process becomes the most important thing in the world for me. Free from email, SMS, distractions and other responsibilities, these far-looking plans are dusted off, reviewed and analysed to be updated or rewritten – the goal is to design what I want to happen in my life over the next 1000 days. I call it the 1000 because inevitably whatever is further than three years out forms more of a wish list, not subject to any real immediate action other than possibly some high-level milestones within the first 1000 days. The focus always ends up on what the next 1000 days entail, with a strong weighting towards the first half of that.

A few weeks before I start work on the 1000, I let anyone I'm working with know that shortly I'll be totally checked out for a few weeks – sometimes, a month or more. For it to work well, it's important to give people a lot of warning that I really expect to be off the grid. With the help of a few late nights I clear the email inboxes and get all overdue tasks done; about two weeks before the break begins, I *stop* taking new tasks on and put an auto-responder in my email to let people know I'm going to be very slow to get back to them for some time. The last week before going offline, I work remotely and start to wind down from daily tasks to slow the flow of requests hopefully to near a halt. I give my team and people I'm working with a time slot each week that they can call me to cover a batch of issues they may have . . . and then I jump offline.

From there, this is what my time looks like over the course of two or so weeks:

- Firstly, try to do absolutely nothing for a day or two.
- Next, sit down and make a long list of all the things I want to achieve during this period – invariably the list is too long and I need to rank what *must* get done. I also collate things I might have thought of or kept as notes in the last few months since I last sat down to do this exercise and look at whatever was still on the list from the last planning period.
- Revisit my existing master list of all the goals or ideas I have – this is kind of like the 'back list' or bucket list that keeps rolling on, continually being updated year after year, and sits within

my black Smythson notebooks, which I reread from cover to cover.

- Define which items move up in priority to be addressed in the coming years as definite goals, and by when I should target making them happen. Brainstorm ideas against the items in this list and anything else that's troubling me or inspiring me. No rules and anything goes before I start to refine down my choices.

- Cut the list into those quick wins that can be reasonably achieved within a year, separate those that are longer term and need to be broken down further.

- Cut each of those lists further, ranking the importance and impact I place on each – asking myself, if I was *forced* to choose an order, which one would I want to do the most?

- For each of the items that make the cut, I put a few bullets down that resemble a high-level milestone plan and be very specific about the *action steps* that are needed to be taken to move each forward into 100-day chunks.

- The rest of the items that didn't make the cut go back on the wish-list backburner and are reviewed next time around or axed.

- The list of goals is then broken down into major milestones to achieve against the four quarters of the year – March, June, September and December.

The 100

These one-year goals are reviewed four times a year over a couple of days, and have a quarterly outlook (i.e. four periods of roughly 100 days) and are further broken down into whatever needs to take place during that period to move things along each month.

The 30

Every 90 days these plans get broken down further into monthly plans at the beginning of each month (i.e. what needs to happen this month to keep things trucking along?). I might spend half a day on creating these plans.

The 10

For a few hours, four Sundays or Mondays a month, I look 10 days ahead and ensure all the weekly goals (including both weekends) are contributing towards the ladder of 30, 100 and so on — I try to list the top three to five things that the week *must* achieve. I print out 10 days of my iCal calendar and use the paper as my physical reminder of what my overarching schedule and plans look like. I also update and print my online task list, which I have used to divide all tasks into various urgency levels, projects and contexts.

Each week those goals get broken down into events and tasks for the 10 days ahead on my task list and I try to *schedule* the times that I'll do them, no differently from dinner with a friend or a doctor's appointment. Write it down, it exists – but schedule it and it *will get done*. I schedule multi-hour blocks within my calendar of either workflow or context. Workflow is where I might sit down and only work on things to do with a certain project or outcome – for example, writing this book. The tricky thing when you get down to 'The 1' is that you can view your to-do list through several lenses; the two I just referred to, and then lastly the time lens, i.e. what is due today, tomorrow and the day after. Balancing all three lenses and being able to view things through them is critical for me to get the most out of my time.

Context, for example, might be physical, mental or digital – such as being at the computer online, doing emails, meeting with people, being in the mode of just 'getting things done' versus going somewhere quiet to just *think*. I find that powering through in the same context – e.g. processing emails – makes me much faster when I dedicate blocks of time to that context, and more importantly, as the minutes tick on, your effectiveness in that context gets better and more meaningful than for example if I just kept picking up and responding to emails every 20 minutes for five minutes at a time, always trying to find time to 'get to them'.

For example, some of my current contextual blocks include: five hours on Monday afternoon for internal communication and meetings, five hours on Thursday afternoon for external communication and meetings, all of Friday morning for my 'white space' to spend time on working or planning my personal development and goals; all of Friday afternoon for long-range strategic planning of my businesses or other activities. There's even time loosely there to deal with *unscheduled* things that come up – as they always do – four hours on Tuesday afternoon is just left blank, knowing it will be filled in. I'm looking for freedom within a framework. It's a guideline, not a rule – some weeks follow the framework, some weeks I just do whatever I want.

The 1

Day to day, I just get things done based on what was decided for the 10. Things move around in the 1 but that's OK because they are all structured within the things that need to be done for the week. So if something slips from Monday to Tuesday – or comes from Thursday to Wednesday – it's all right as long as each day you've got one eye on the 1 and the other on the 10.

START WITH A VERB

Every big idea needs to be broken down into sub-steps that need to happen before you can achieve the higher-order goal of what you were trying to write down. When breaking down larger goals into smaller chunks, ultimately there comes a point where you need to decide 'what next?' At this point, where you turn something into a 'to do' or an action step, it's vital to start how you describe it with a *verb* as that represents what you actually have to *do* to make this happen. If you don't it's just a stream of consciousness written down on paper. A list without verbs is impotent. Verbs are easily able to be shared and people become accountable when you are working in team environments because a verb is much more black and white than just words. If you can't break something into a statement beginning with a verb, then you have not broken it down enough to be actionable.

As a simple example – if 'buy a home' is on your list, even though 'buy' is a verb, that's a goal, not a task. It needs to be broken down into tasks such as: decide on budget; decide on area; decide on timing. For each of those milestones they need to be further broken down – to decide on the budget you need to sit down and review your current budget and allocate a portion to the house. How much you need to break things down depends a lot on how much you know about a subject and how many shortcuts you can take towards the goal or task.

PROTECTING WEEKLY PERSONAL SPACE

In addition to that regime, every week I have time carved out – Friday mornings – when I'm totally unplugged and focused entirely on *thinking*. It takes a lot for anybody to wrestle that time from me – I use part of it to see how I'm tracking against the 100- and 30-day plans, but mostly to work on habits and invest in self-development. I might ask myself why I approached something the way I did in the recent week, or deconstruct successes and failures and review the values that I have committed myself to.

I picked up this last habit – probably the most important one of all of them – from Benjamin Franklin, who created a personal scorecard to grade himself on what he called the 13 'virtues' that he aspired to embody. Each week he planned to focus on one virtue, and if he successfully lived it then a tick was marked, and if not, a cross. His aim was to complete a full year with nothing but ticks. The important point here is that no matter how busy you think you are, you can always find and protect sacred time in a sacred place to *meet with yourself*. If Benjamin Franklin could find the time, so can you.

WHAT WORKS FOR YOU

The exercise above is designed to cover potentially every aspect of your life: where you want to travel; languages you want to learn; skills you want to acquire; things you want to own; restaurants you want to open; books you want to write; children you want to have. I have used this method to make the necessary plans to learn how to sail; to write this book; to start new companies and close old ones; to leave a job; to read dozens of books lying waiting for me on my shelf; to get a new passport on time and to be there to see the All Blacks win the Rugby World Cup.

But this doesn't mean that it will work for you. Whatever the system you use to turn your dreams or goals into reality — no matter how big or small they are — you *need* to have one, and you need to personalise it so that it works for you. The more you improve it, the better it will serve you as long as you commit to it until it becomes habit.

THINKING

DIFFERENT

There was debate between Steve Jobs and some of his colleagues who argued that the grammar around the Apple slogan 'Think Different' should have been Think Differently. Jobs argued that what he meant was not 'go and think differently', but Think Different, the noun, like some people might say 'Think Black' or 'Think Money' – he meant Think *Different*.

Is it magical, raw talent to be able to think different – or can you bottle it? Maybe you can't, but here are a few ways to try:

DESIGN THINKING

As a design and architecture student I was trained in what some people might call the design thinking process: divergent and convergent thinking. You start broad – creative, conceptual and inspirational – and diverge outwards. Then you narrow down – refine, structured, detail – and converge inwards. You harness the power of ideas and manage them through freedom within a framework to push them through a funnel, squeezing out the best of them, and then squeezing out the best from the best to get you to the point of finality.

Getting stuck in either mode is risky – you either create too many ideas and drown, or create too few and limit yourself. Sometimes you need to create no constraints and let anything flow and allow the ideas to tumble from the sky, before switching modes, tightening the constraints with limits and boundaries. New ways to think about things will be forced out under those conditions.

Everyone can create a process that helps them diverge and converge in their thinking, but the quality of the ideas that come out might still be poor. And even if they are good ideas, they might not be unique. And even if they're unique they might not be uniquely *yours*. So how do you get good ideas that look like they're uniquely yours?

Borrow and steal

Nothing truly new exists — you can start from here. There are no new ideas in the world. What's different or original is how people put pieces together — what contemporary people do with historical knowledge. Sometimes the idea lies in the past and was just ahead of its time; or was undiscovered or not promoted so nobody alive today has ever really known it. Sometimes it's the future, but as the future is often already here — just not evenly distributed — it's about the timing of when an idea is ready to be born and what the conditions are that make it possible to spread.

We can always look to borrow and steal from the past to help shape the future. History is littered with new and original ideas that died not because they were bad, but because they were born in the wrong era, or born from the wrong author. The irony of 'new ideas' is that you must borrow and steal to create uniqueness. I don't mean plagiarising — if you create a carbon copy, you must credit and reference your source. I mean borrowing from inspiration. Your thoughts are the children of your inspiration.

Fuse inspiration

When you see something you like, you need to pause and think about exactly what it is about it that moves and inspires you. It's almost a waste of inspiration not to pick through the whole to dissect the parts that wink straight at you and call out your name. If we are too careless with our relationship with what inspires us, we might fail to know exactly what speaks to us, to know how to easily pick it off the shelf to use it again when we need it.

What makes ideas uniquely *somebody*'s is how they have synthesised what they knew or found, mixing and matching the parts that resonate with them in a way that only they can. We are the synthesis of all we have been influenced by and borrowed from. So if your palette is narrow, and your inspiration vague, your thoughts will be bland and blurred. If your palette blends west and east, young and old, history and future and picks out the details that hide within them, you won't be able to help having a far greater texture of interesting ideas. You'll naturally see things from so many angles that you'll be forced to mash them up and spit out your own take.

If you channel just one set of inspiration you will be seen as a fake – trying to be something you are not. If you channel 50 inspirations spanning five centuries you will be forced to fuse them together, to reconcile those influences in such a way that what comes out of it is uniquely yours.

Be curious

Be curious. There's often *no good reason* why things are the way they are. Things are the way they are because nobody has changed them yet. Take nothing for granted. Look at every problem as an opportunity. Never malign the problem, espouse the solution. Rethink things from where they are towards where they can be. And if you feel strongly enough about it, *you* should change it. People wanting to change things have created revolutions – in products, society, art and culture – since time began. Keep up the tradition.

Be prolific

Start with more. To get flowing, and to draw energy into producing consistently better ideas, produce more of them. Write down a new idea each day. Or write five. Let them pass, and write more the next day – the better the thoughts you have, the harder it is to get wedded to any of them. If you have one really different thought, and attach yourself to it, it closes out the possibilities of others. If you have three different thoughts, and need to pick one, you either *have* to come up with a better idea, or make one of those three stand out. Be prolific to keep raising the bar.

The majority of people are incapable of original thinking because they are unable to escape from the tyranny of reason.

David Ogilvy

Be careful how you validate

Where do you get your validation from? How much are you willing to depend on the judgment of others? How do you check if a thought you have is good?

Be careful who you test new ideas with, because not everybody has the capacity to critique them and absorb them.

What's at stake here?

Why is it important to think different? It's who you are. It's about independence versus second-handedness. It's your stamp on the world. You can choose to be happy with a stamp that is like everybody else's or develop one that clearly defines *you*. To be able to speak up with your thoughts – the thoughts that are different – you need to have the private confidence to be public. Get uncomfortable. If you're not uncomfortable, you're not pushing hard enough.

II

09

Chips

What to do? Yes.

How? Yes.

When? Yes.

Where? Yes.

Why?

No idea, really.

The thing I know now that I didn't know then was that I had no idea why I decided the things I had decided, and when I came home from the world tour in July 2003, I didn't particularly care either. It didn't seem to matter. I charged ahead anyway. I pulled out some of the $1 million or so in chips to play with, and started to put them down. I wanted to get into the bar business, so down went a few and I bought half the Crow Bar, where I spent almost every drinking hour; just for good measure, a little while later, I tossed a few more down and co-founded a vodka distribution company to sell Kiwi vodka in Asia. I wanted to be in the fashion industry, so out came more chips, and I stacked them up neatly behind a new cashmere clothing label I helped start called *To Sir With Love*; I wanted to create a consumer brand so I splayed out still more chips and started a venture to repackage the *I Heart NY* brand as *I Heart NZ*. All of these bets and more were placed within about 12 or 18 very short months and all for what I thought were very good reasons.

From having nothing to do and nowhere to be, all of a sudden I was busy, and in a rush with about six places to be and 60 things to do. But I still really had *no* idea why I was doing any of it all.

In 2004, at the height of this schizophrenia, one of these places I was to be at was of course The Hyperfactory, the company we had started at the beginning of it all. Geoffrey was charging ahead knocking on doors, selling the idea of how SMS text messaging was becoming a marketing tool — a way for brands to interact with people, a way for radio and television channels to engage live with their invisible users for the first time to send messages to the DJ, to vote which music video they wanted to see. He was good and we were onto something and people were really starting to buy it. I began to spend more and more time with him to grow the business. By this time my younger brother Calum had started to drop out of university and drop into the office, making it a family affair. Soon after, we made our first hires in Darnell, Brani and Srini — like a lot of the people who joined us, they were eventually caught up in the adventure and (almost) never left.

In those really early days we made a pact: wherever we go in the world, we'll be the best. We'll predict and create the future and have others follow our lead. We'll sell vision and ideas first and figure out how to make them happen later. If people think it's impossible, we'll prove them wrong. And every single year, we'll do something nobody has ever technically achieved before. These became the unwritten rules of our culture, and of our family.

But New Zealand wasn't the place to limit these dreams to. We wanted to grow up and break out of Auckland and prove we could sit at the big-boy table in the global capitals of the world. With mobile usage and technologies Asia was far ahead of the rest of the world and seemed like a logical place to be, and Hong Kong seemed like a logical place to start. There were a lot of people, they had a lot of phones, and apparently they had a lot of money too. The New York of the Far East, its skyscrapers, billionaires and the gateway to China — Hong Kong would be the key to unlock our fame, fortune and fantasy.

I formed a plan, we stacked a chunk of the remaining chips we had left behind it, raised a bit more funding to give us enough gas in the tank and were ready to push. But who was going to do the pushing?

With about six businesses on the go and an idea to move back to Hong Kong, in one of the craziest things I've ever done, I left Maya and moved up there to set up the outpost. The same Maya who had stuck by me when shades of blue turned black in October 2000. The same Maya who stood by me when Feverpitch shot into the sky just to come crashing back down again less than two years later. The same Maya who never flinched, who said that those things didn't matter and we'd get through it all.

My thesis was that if Maya and I were meant to be then we needed to test it. I worried that university romances that continued forever never really got a taste of the real world and we would always look back wondering 'what if?', blaming one another for the lack of freedom and experimentation and adventures. Today, relationships happen so fast and we live so long that maybe I felt that putting them to extreme tests early would either forge them into lifelong unity or break them just a little earlier than they would have broken anyway.

Let's agree that my relationship philosophy was unorthodox. Some would call it stupid. It was definitely an enormous risk. So it

We separated. I believed that the world was too small for us not to find our way back if we were meant to. I've never sky jumped — I don't like physical risks — but I imagine this is what it feels like, the faith you need, the danger you knowingly walk into and the exhilaration you expect to follow.

I packed.

I left.

I jumped.

I landed.

I must have stayed in a hotel my first nights in Hong Kong — I have no recollection of those first days. I began doing what I knew I was good at — starting things. I got a flat, an office and some furniture. I incorporated a company, opened bank accounts, bought a cellphone, internet access, computers. I set us up. It was mundane stuff but one by one I ticked it all off and we were in business.

While this was all going on I was living in Starbucks, interviewing candidates to join the journey, and I hired our first man on the ground. We started work, picked up the phones and began calling people. Life in Hong Kong the second time around was very different. I had few close friends, I'd lost my rudder in Maya and quickly began drinking too much and sleeping too little.

The work was moving in the right direction, but not exactly according to plan. Our clients were all advertising agencies who just weren't getting it. They didn't see that mobile was the future of interaction, that it was to be the entirety of the traditional worlds of media and marketing that they knew well, all rolled into one; that it was to be the television and radio, the internet and magazines, the email and flyers packed into a tiny device that goes in your jacket, your jeans or your jersey pocket. They didn't understand that this device was on the cusp of becoming the remote control to our lives. And they didn't care, at least not like we did. Why should they? They got paid to make television ads and glossy print ads for magazines, not experiences to live on a two-inch screen.

I'm making it sound like nobody wanted to know us. Don't get me wrong — they did. We made plenty of friends; they *loved* to hear from us and see our shiny new ideas that they would show to their clients, the big brands of the world, to make *them* look good. To expect them to actually push a little though, and try and sell those ideas for us, was too hard. People don't do things when they're too hard — and to try and create the future is bloody difficult. To have the faith to buy the future from somebody *else* is maybe even harder; people, in general, would rather just focus on the present and take fewer risks. So our ideas became like the sweets you get at the end of a restaurant meal — you love them, and you'll eat them if they're sitting there, but you don't expect to pay for them. Getting our ideas sold was like pushing shit uphill. If the ideas never got sold, we couldn't sell our tech; if we couldn't sell our tech, we couldn't make a margin; if we couldn't make a margin, we couldn't pay the rent; if we couldn't pay the rent, we would be out of business.

I figured the problem wasn't with us — it was with them. Of course it was. How could we have been so dumb? As the months wore on and the convincing wasn't converting, we needed to try something different. We needed to make something big happen or we'd be hacking away in Hong Kong for years to no end. When things aren't going to plan and problems seem to be mounting, I try to see what they might look like if we made them bigger. So towards the end of 2004 I took our little Hong Kong problem and tried to turn it into a global one. We thought maybe that the way to make our small problem a big problem was to tell our story to the biggest person who would listen — the person who would be the most concerned that this might be *their* problem, not just ours — to ensure *they* didn't miss a tidal wave coming from behind. My brother and I sat around the table one day with a brainwave.

'If these guys in Hong Kong don't get it, perhaps we need to get to their boss's boss's boss, who will want to know. Somebody who will be concerned that the team on the ground don't "get" something that's about to change the way we all communicate. We need to get to the very top of an agency that will want to lead; an agency who will want to be out in front.'

'So who do we think are the top three?'

We made a list of a few top agencies and the people who ran them, and how we might get to them. We ranked who we wanted to speak with.

'I'd say Ogilvy is up there; we can get in easily enough to see somebody. And TBWA would be up there; Hubert knows the Chairman of A-Pac.'

'OK, so let's say they're number two and number three, and let's go after them — but who is the most famous?'

'Saatchi & Saatchi.'

'Kind of impossible.'

'So let's try,' we both agreed.

Saatchi & Saatchi is the world's most famous advertising agency and is arguably the only one that even the man in the street has heard of; it is one of the largest and has 8000 staff in over 100 offices around the world. We approached the other people and companies all over Asia and tried any route to get to big dogs

— but our number-one target became Saatchi & Saatchi, and our highest priority was a sit-down with their global boss Kevin Roberts, who we did not know and had never met. We had done some work with their tiny office in New Zealand and they had a visionary and assertive creative director there, Tom Eslinger, who Geoffrey knew. After exploring a myriad of possible routes to get to Kevin, we discovered he had links to New Zealand; after a further four weeks I discovered that the best link to him so far was sitting right inside my Hong Kong apartment.

It was like knowing where the string was tied to at the end, and having to walk backwards to connect the dots to somewhere that you were already connected to. My flatmate in Hong Kong, Charlotte Glennie, was the inspirational Television New Zealand Asia correspondent at the time and it just so happened that her brother or mother, who I didn't know, knew Kevin's sons — or something. I can't quite remember the connection, but it was tenuous. I politely begged her to somehow get us in for the coveted 15 minutes. Somehow she made it happen and a few weeks before Christmas 2004 we had a slot on his schedule.

When you watch dramatic movies of the young guy or girl striving to climb the ladder of life, and the protagonist gets their break — their shot at a life-changing event — your heart races for them as the devastation you feel if they screw it up can only be rivalled by the elation if they nail it. Let me share something I have learned. These moments you see on television and in the movies, where the lead character needs to come through — these turning points — are in fact real. Often they come down to having one, five or 15 minutes to make an impression, to convince somebody to do something, and that you are the right person for them to take a gamble on. Steve Jobs spoke of leaving a dent in the universe. When you meet certain people, you want to do your

Whenever I run into a problem I can't solve, I always make it bigger.

Dwight D. Eisenhower

unrelenting best to leave a dent in their memory. We were about to walk into one such meeting.

We had our 15 minutes with Kevin Roberts, head of the most famous advertising agency in the entire world. For that 15 minutes we had prepared for about four weeks. We'd distilled what we wanted to say into 10 large-format pages in a huge flipbook. We used a big font, crisply hand-drawn images, a handful of critical statistics and beautifully drawn charts; just 10 pages in all. Our story was designed to be told in five minutes. One image that I remember vividly: the back jeans pocket of a young girl, with what looked like an iPod sticking out, but on it clearly said 'iPhone'. The Apple star was just starting to rise again with the phenomenal success of the iPod — you could tell the brand was on a trajectory towards global cult status and they were *not* a client of Saatchi & Saatchi and yet were arguably the most coveted client in the industry. The flipbook was finished in the first weeks of December 2004; the iPhone would not be announced until January 2007.

We arrived. Just like the movies we were left to wait for what seemed like forever, but was probably only 40 minutes. All of a sudden we were led past the brick walls and wide timber stairs down to the basement office to be greeted by Kevin dressed in his customary streamlined black.

Showtime.

We sat. Fifteen seconds of pleasantries. And then straight out of a Hollywood script he opened.

'You have fifteen minutes.'

We sat. We pulled out the flipbook and we walked him through it page by page, pausing only to check he was following. Weeks of work and thinking was being told in a story of no more than five minutes. A story that went something like this:

If you can't say it in five minutes, you don't know what you're saying.

'You are the greatest storytellers in the world for the greatest brands in the world; the future of stories and experiences is shifting from television and radio to online and the internet.

The future beyond this is telling stories and helping consumers live better lives through your brands, through their handsets. These devices that we think of as phones today will become the remote controls to our world tomorrow; brands need to know how to navigate this landscape, and nobody does — including you.

We do.

We are the best in the world.

Here are our world-first innovations, and our clients and our awards to show for it. We are local, you are global; we want to be global. We are small, you are large; we want to be large. You are slow, we are fast; you want to be fast. You have 8000 people; we have 10. Let us stand on your shoulders and be your global partners in these key cities around the world. All you do is open doors, give us a seat to sit in and let us walk in with you. You will look good, and we will both do well.

You will have the best experts within your family, at no cost to you, and we will have the chance to go global and get big.

What do you say?'

If I have seen further it is by standing on the shoulders of Giants.

Sir Isaac Newton

10

Forks

If they say life doesn't come down to moments, let me tell you they are lying. If they say that it's not what you know, it's who you know, let me tell you there's truth written left to right within those words. If they say that it's not the number of breaths you take but it's the number of moments that take your breath away, they're not off base. *But* when you get presented with these moments, and you are there ready to live them, let me suggest that what matters above all is that you put your undivided energy and consciousness into them with confidence and optimism, and that you expend every ounce of spiritual, mental and physical capacity you have, to come out the other side with the outcome you want.

At certain points life gets a big push from who you know, not what you know. At certain junctures life absolutely does come down to critical moments — but the secret to it all is to *take* them with both hands and a full heart, and *make them happen.* When you encounter or create these moments what you are facing are the forks in your path that will totally change the trajectory of an idea, a career, a company, a relationship, a life, a movement. What you *do* in those moments — at the fork — means everything.

The flipbook was shut.

The story told.

The 15 minutes up.

Kevin rose from the couch and ended our meeting. A black silhouette glided across the timber floors towards his desk. He spoke.

'What I do, boys, is open doors. What you do after that is up to you.'

We waited.

'Can I keep this?' he said, holding up our pitch.

'Of course.'

'Meet Jim O'Mahoney in Sydney. You've passed my sniff test. Let's see what you can do.'

That was it.

Geoffrey and I took this to mean that 15 minutes after we walked in that door it was up to us if we were to become Saatchi & Saatchi's global partner to show them and their clients the way of the future. Well if it was up to us, of course it was going to happen.

Some people think of this story as inspiring. It is. It still inspires *me* when I look back and think of it. It is inspiring that a man who runs the most famous advertising agency in the world trusts his gut and builds a case to make decisions quickly, on the spot, based on stories and people. Decisions he knows can change the course of a young kid's life. It's also inspiring to think that us two brothers trundled up there with our eight-person army behind us, gave it a shot and had the courage to suggest that we should be the global minnow partner of a giant, believing what we were saying with every fibre of our being.

As inspiring as these moments are to encounter or create, what can be truly inspiring is what you do with them. What are the lessons? Does this mean it's all who you know — just rock up

Show me where to stand and I'll move the world.

Archimedes

and shake hands and off you go? Does this mean that whenever you get a big moment you just cut the line and make it happen?

Did I mention we spent weeks prepping for these 15 minutes? Weeks. We probably spent one day of prep per minute of meeting. Did I mention we agonised over every word, every drawing, every chart? It was one of the most well-prepared presentations my brother and I have ever done — but was that more important or was it the spirit we went in with? The spirit of what's in it for the *other* guy? What gift can we offer? We started from the opposite of what we wanted and from a place of what could we give — how can we build this in such a way that makes it very, very difficult for him to refuse?

Our small problems were on a path to disappearing because we had created newer, bigger ones. Now we had some heavyweight partners: Jim and Kevin. They saw the same problem as us: Saatchi & Saatchi had no ability to predict the future in mobile and look like they knew what they were doing. Having achieved the seemingly impossible, after seeing in the 2005 New Year, I left Auckland and returned to Hong Kong.

Sometimes thinking the impossible means convincing just one person — the right person. Sometimes it means convincing the masses. Sometimes it means both — what people might call top down and bottom up. Whatever you are dreaming of, if it involves great change or disruption, you have to consider where the leverage points are and how you use them to make great things happen.

What Archimedes was speaking of was leverage and levers. He understood that when you knew the levers that created change, and you could create the fulcrum, all you had to do was stand, with all the pressure you could muster, on the lever at the end of the fulcrum. Another analogy to this is acupressure — when you know where the pressure points are, you focus on those points and ignore everything else. Kevin was our lever; Saatchi was our fulcrum.

A short while later I got a slot on Jim's calendar and had to get to Australia to see him for an hour to seal a deal. Six thousand kilometres for a 60-minute meeting; then six thousand kilometres right back again. My dad always told me to get on planes — see people; have a beer; make connections. So I've never ever had a problem flying around the world to see somebody for an hour. If I believe it will create one of those forks in the road, I will fly around the world to sit with somebody for 15 minutes. The world is a lot smaller than people tend to think and when people know that you have made the effort to come all the way *just* to meet them, they will either think you are wildly unpredictable or that you really value the chance to. Either of those impressions is fine with me.

Although we were always running lean on cash, there are times where it makes all the sense in the world to do the nonsensical thing and I felt this trip to Sydney was one of them. I wanted to arrive there in the fashion that I expected to leave. From years of only ever flying economy, I used every air point I had in one hit for a first-class return flight on Qantas. It was my mental commitment that this meeting *had* to go very well, Jim and I were going to get along, and then, in a few years I might be worrying about a menagerie of things, but having enough air points was not going to be one of them.

A few months later we signed a simple three-page deal, confirming the spirit and salient points of what we had outlined in the flipbook. We started to build on it and knock on Saatchi doors around the region.

By thinking bigger — and in this case as big as we could — we had carved a totally new path and shared the problem with a powerful ally: a problem shared became a problem halved. Lines began to open, first Hong Kong, then Sydney, Singapore and of course, Auckland. In 2005 we built our journey around the partnership as Jim and Kevin opened up the network to us. *Nothing* came to us on a platter. And nothing happened *just* because Jim or Kevin said so — the only reason we made it work was that we busted on through and gave it everything. We gave and we gave and we gave. Wherever we were asked to be, we went. Whatever we were asked to do we did. There was no cost to them. We believed that if we did well, if we showed that we were of value and committed, time and again, that when the time came, people started to 'get it' and clients would tip, we could be there to catch the work and get what we'd earned. We believed that by doing the right thing over and over again, the right thing would eventually happen to us.

Word soon spread within the network and we received an invitation to fly to New York to present to a September summit being held with the bosses of regional offices from all around the world — the United States, China, England, Italy, Brazil and beyond.

Geoffrey and I prepared to head over and visit New York together. We arrived really late and (as most tourists do) stayed in Times Square in the cheapest hotel we could afford. We looked up Sparks Steak House and walked over for a late-night steak at the legendary joint where one of the last mob bosses of the Gambino mafia family, Big Paulie Castellano, was gunned down right outside on the street. We'd seen the famous picture of him sprawled across the sidewalk and wanted to check the place out for ourselves. The steakhouses in New York are unrivalled — in a large crimson-lit room the old-timer server wheeled the steaks in on a huge cart and offered us all sorts of accoutrements to choose from. We bought a 'Sparks' mug and steak knife to record the occasion, waded through the neon-glazed oppressive cage that is midtown Manhattan and went to sleep. According to Sinatra we were about to be tested as to whether we could make it 'anywhere' — and the next day was one more of those moments that would open up to create another fork in the road.

We pulled up to 375 Hudson in lower Manhattan and took the guest elevator that had 'Nothing's Impossible' emblazoned across the walls in white on black. On the sixteenth floor, expansive floor-to-ceiling glass windows surrounded the lobby with views over Manhattan. The famous work for famous brands hung proudly along the inner walls and played on the screens. A few formalities. A few introductions and not long after, we slipped into an inner room and went on show once again.

Geoffrey and I kicked into gear. We laid out our expansive vision of the future and showed them what we were doing in Asia with video, games, television and content *all* through cellular phones on pilot projects with brands like McDonald's and adidas. The message was simple: all this is coming to a town near you and you can lead, follow or risk looking foolish by ignoring it.

They'd never seen anything like it. We looked like we came from the future — and to be fair, we had — given that what was going on in Asia was *years* ahead of what America would expect to encounter any time soon. We played off each other as we always do together and came to a close, faced with varied expressions across the room. Well?

The discerning audience was an uneasy blend of convinced and bemused. The bemused among them struggled to see how what we were doing had any impact on their future. 'Phones? We make television ads.' Remember, this was the summer of 2005 — the iPhone was still but a sketch in our flipbook, almost every European and American used their phone just for calling; if they were right up with the play they might have used it to send a text message every now and then but to really imagine what the world looked like with the power of mobile devices you had to have a bit of creativity and cast your eyes out three or five years into the future. The convinced understood we were on the cusp of a revolution in the way people consumed media, accessed the internet and connected with friends and information they needed.

After three days in New York we flew out. Geoffrey headed for the West Coast en route to New Zealand and I took the 16-hour direct flight to Hong Kong. Before we left, the New York bosses thanked us for making the trip all the way to see them; they politely told us that if we ever wanted to come back, they would make room. Later that evening in the dim tan and beige shadow of a midtown hotel room, we thought to ourselves — *could* we make it here? Really?

I started to list all the reasons why it was a bad idea. Well I'd have to get a visa to live in America, which would be virtually impossible to come by and surely very expensive; I'd have to get a place to live, which costs a fortune in Manhattan; I'd be in a totally different time zone to the headquarters in New Zealand; I'd be out on my own in a country I'd never been in before, where I didn't know a soul and was thousands of kilometres from my nearest relative; I had barely started in Hong Kong a year ago so who would pick up the pieces there? And lastly, America was never part of the plan. It wasn't what the investors had backed; we knew it was too expensive, too risky and too much of an unknown; in short, it was impractical. And impossible. But wait. Hang on. If it's impossible . . .

Back in Hong Kong, the adrenalin of the challenge of America and the scale of the opportunity drove me over the edge. For the first time in a long time I felt a drive that would motivate me through hell and back. A few days passed and I called up Geoffrey and my father to talk it through.

It seemed just days later that I booked a ticket and packed up my trusty, tiny Delsey suitcase covered in airport and airline markings from London to Las Vegas — my Paddington Bear case, after the bear who travelled from Peru to Paddington Station in Michael Bond's childhood stories, and it had gone everywhere with me since university. I left almost all of my personal things behind and as the oppressive summer of Hong Kong was dying down, Paddington and I were off to New York to meet an oppressive winter about to start. Barely a month after that arrival celebration at Spark's Steak House I was back; I had booked five nights in a hotel — from night six I had no plan, and not a lot of money. No visa, no home, no friends, and a suitcase of summer clothes.

My move to New York was a well-calculated risk that Dad and Geoffrey agreed with. I would take my credit cards, and rack up to $10,000, which I figured would last for three or four months. If I couldn't score a client by then, we would all reassess. If I did, we knew that this was the window we'd been waiting for and we needed to push all the chips we had left on America; we would raise more capital to double down and take the gamble of our lives by hiring a sales guy and a project manager in New York, which would cost US$20,000 a month at least, about what Geoffrey and I paid ourselves for an entire year.

Leap and the net will appear.

My only contacts were a few people I'd met at Saatchi, but I felt fearless and confident. I'd come from the future and was here to sell it. I went about setting up shop all over again. The Saatchi people carved me out a space on the eighteenth floor of their building and I moved in. In one pouring night of rain I trekked over to view my first sublease apartment, barely bigger than Keiji's in Tokyo. It was in a walk-up building in the West Village and I signed up for it on the spot. Winter was setting in and I'd barely spared the time to kit myself out; the worst snowstorm in years struck the city, dumping 50 cm in Central Park one evening and turning lower Manhattan into a white desert with mounds and valleys of pristine powder disguising the sidewalks from the roads, the hydrants from the cars and the parks from the flowerbeds.

As much as I was just trying to settle in, I was worried too about all of my 'children'. Now spread across three continents, I had no time to keep up with any of them. By the time I'd pushed out and punched through a New York day I couldn't stay awake another New York minute to talk cashmere, vodka or bars to my partners in Hong Kong, Auckland or Sydney. Stretched across both ends of the global time-and-date line, bed was on my mind long before I was off the phone.

I somehow thought I could do it all, so I *would* do it all. Maybe I thought it might make me feel important, creative, excited? Maybe I thought I'd feel like a proud parent with many doting children, taking them to football practice, guitar lessons, swimming and French class — packing it all in so I could tell my fellow parents of all the great things little Johnny was doing? Maybe.

From such clarity in the streets of Paris just a few years before, how did I end up in this chaos? With my multiple ventures across multiple continents, I was now chasing a portfolio life like the ones I'd read about but wasn't able to handle. That is to say, I didn't have the maturity, confidence or skills to manage what I'd built for myself, and most importantly, I didn't have the *people*. I had no concept of the *team* required to run a life like this, scattered across so many experiments and new ideas. It was all slowly beginning to crush me — under the test of time zones and distance, the diffusion of energy and distractions, and a little too much bourbon and beer — one by one the plates I had started spinning began to wobble. Naïve and reluctant to do the brutally hard work required to get each one of them to where I thought I wanted to be, and unwilling to start small, focus on one thing and build — the collision of demands on my time, ego and energy marked the beginning of an instructive period of learning how *not* to live and work.

Alight with plenty of goals and what I *thought* was a purpose I ended up feeling more and more like a spectator of my own experiment, forcing so hard to do the right thing, with things refusing to come out right. I knew something was very out of balance.

After my time in Europe, I had quickly created a framework, a container, for all the things I wanted in life (which was totally fine), but even quicker than that, I had stuffed things in it that I'd thought about for only weeks or months (which were now starting to come unstuck). I knew how important it was to have that framework — and still do, because you *have* to have a plan, and you need to know what you want to make it happen — but I think I was learning just as fast that it's far more important to be careful about the things you try to put in it. They all looked right on paper. Right for somebody — but maybe not right for me. When you can do *anything* the mistake is to do everything.

Doing everything is not a good plan, because everything we do defines us every bit as much as everything we don't.

I thought I was too smart to make that mistake, but it turns out I wasn't. Doing everything is not a good plan, because everything we do defines us every bit as much as everything we don't.

The mind works like a GPS, I am certain of it. If you focus consistently enough on the things you want and convince yourself persistently enough that you will get them, all of a sudden they appear and sometimes you learn you didn't really want them at all. They arrive, one after the other, tumbling on top of you and royally messing up your shit. They may be sent by the universe to teach you a lesson to not be so greedy or impatient. They may even be sent just to test you — can you handle it?

I think we all feel there is a voice inside us we are trying to find, a calling — what we are put here to do, what life we are put here to live. I thought I'd half-figured that out in Paris, although I hadn't really, I'd just figured out a few ideas. I thought I was on my way but, no, far from it. I now wanted to pull down *all* these pieces I had built up all around me just to match the plan I'd written for myself and I realised that yes, it was just one more set of tests. Tests to force me to question, is this *really* what you want? Because you asked for it, so here it is.

With the goals I'd set at first — the money, the businesses — I now thought much of what I'd written down back then wasn't what I really believed or needed. It was what I *thought* I believed or needed. Because I had chosen to be an entrepreneur and that was my course in life, from all that I had read, from all that I had heard I was convinced that *in business*, success was defined by how much money I made. It was how I would be measured, and so I set my goals.

Now, there's nothing inherently wrong with wanting to be rich. I didn't think that then, and I don't think it now. But I have never dreamed that having *things* would make life better, and I've never been the type of person who wanted one of everything — I'd sooner have less than more. I'd just picked a number, based on the cold, hard, impersonal reality of it being a number. But now I was beginning to doubt how important that number even was.

I now knew one more thing: never to get involved in five ventures at once. Not on my own. So one by one I wound them back or sold out. The only way I was going to survive here in New York was by focusing entirely on The Hyperfactory and getting the job done. Which is what I started to do.

Within a few months of pitching every single day we scored a major client. Johnson & Johnson is one of the biggest companies in the world; financially the deal was larger and more profitable than any other project we'd ever sold. Their brand Tylenol was a sponsor of the Mexican team in the upcoming FIFA 2006 World Cup; we'd shown them the work we'd done with adidas in Hong Kong to turn their sponsorship of the Real Madrid football team into an entire mobile programme with exclusive clips, interviews, downloads, interaction with the players and guides to the games, all available to people through their phones. Once they saw it they wanted the same thing.

We had agreed to pull the trigger if we hit a winner, so not long after that I hired a hungry young guy from Connecticut named Jeff Arbour and together we unleashed everything we had on America, repeating our mantra that we had come from the future and that we would safely lead the way.

Clients came tumbling in.

Crest toothpaste and Folgers coffee were next — both part of the Procter & Gamble company, the largest packaged goods company in the world. We built little mobile websites for them and created a programme for Folgers customers to create custom wake-up calls sent to their phones.

Motorola followed. The handset manufacturer was on top of the world at the time, and tasked us with creating videos and downloadable guides to every model of their handsets so that new customers could learn how to use all the features of their phones.

Within a year we were known as the best at what we did in America; we *had* come from the future, I had the foreign accent to prove it, and now we had the clients lined up to back up our story. We were turning five years old as a company: five years of credit cards, air miles, overdrafts and hard yards; five years of pain and pressure; five years of ideas and intentions; five years of feigning and praying; five years of believing and steeling ourselves; five years of hiring and firing — and despite all of that, we now knew that the New York gamble marked only the *beginning* of the beginning. We had taken five years to start to become an overnight success.

11

Hollywood

History, as they say, is the rest. And the rest is not that interesting or insightful, to be honest, nor is it that important. It's the moments that create the forks in the road that are key, and what you do with them when they come to you. This was another fork. We picked a path. We gave it everything and pushed through it without looking back.

In the middle of 2006, Maya and I decided that we should give it another go. She made a brave choice filled with sacrifice to move over to America, to a city she'd never even visited. As we weren't married, she came over on a partner visa that prevented her from working, so not only was she uprooting to be alone with me halfway across the world, she was also abandoning her promising advertising career on top of it. Although some people may not consider her a risk-taker, she has never been afraid to swim against the tide. We agreed it was worth a shot, and although I knew for months she was coming, one day it felt like she just 'arrived' in town and I was not ready for her. I'm not going to lie — it was turbulent and New York at the height of the frenzy was a very distracting place to try and fuse fresh flesh over timeworn wounds, but we tried.

At The Hyperfactory we raised several million dollars from a group of New Zealand investors led by Geoff Ross and Grant Baker, who had built a global vodka company called 42 Below and sold it to Bacardi. With cash in the bank we opened offices everywhere — it was like throwing darts at a map — San Francisco, Chicago and Sydney, even a software development centre in Hyderabad, India; as quickly as it must feel like it's unfolding in these pages, we were on our way to a team of 150 people in seven cities around the planet.

Maya and I moved to Los Angeles and set up shop there solely to service Saatchi's key client Toyota and the six-figure deals soon became seven. We moved into one of our investor's offices in Beverly Hills — Rich Frank used to be the head of Disney Studios and was chairman of a celebrity-management company that represented everybody from Martin Scorsese to Britney Spears. Snoop Dogg and his extensive entourage would show up every now and then; OneRepublic, a hit band of the day, would often drop in and bubblegum pop star Mandy Moore was everywhere in the office, on the walls, signed CDs, books and posters.

I was at a conference at the Beverly Hills Hilton in November 2007 and popped out to the cavernous marble lobby to pick up a call from Rich. It was noisy with no quiet spots but I could just make out that he was asking if I wanted to meet with Garth Brooks tomorrow. I didn't know. I held the phone and checked with one of my guys. 'Do I want to meet with Garth Brooks?'

Then I got taken to school. Garth Brooks is the biggest star the world outside of America has never heard of. *Inside* America he is a country music giant and the second biggest-selling solo artist in America after Elvis (or third if you include the Beatles as a band). He's sold 130 million albums, had

14 Grammy nominations, 24 Billboard Awards and was the Recording Industry Association of America Artist of the Century for the 1900s. And tomorrow, he was being recognised as having surpassed Elvis by five million to become the best-selling solo artist in American album history.

'Yes Rich, we want to meet with Garth. I think we do.'

The next day I drove up to Hollywood in our cheap and chic black and tan early nineties Mercedes station wagon, pulled up around the back of Hollywood Boulevard and parked in a garage a few blocks from the famous circular Capitol Records building, where I needed to be in about 20 minutes. It was the middle of the morning on an ordinary day and I walked into the type of chaos that you see on television surrounding Madonna or Justin Bieber. The road was closed, there were police everywhere and screaming fans 15 rows deep behind barricades keeping them out of touching distance of the legend in the cowboy hat who was just metres from his own star on the Hollywood Walk of Fame.

I am slim and small, so I threaded myself through the crowd row by row until I got to the front where Rich said he'd see me. There he was, just as he'd said. A nod and a gesture and the barricade opened up, security ushered me past and I strolled into the building. Upstairs we waited in a room that was split into two with a partition in the middle; Garth was doing television and radio interviews on the other side. Before long he strolled over and gave Rich a bear hug. Rich did his thing, introduced us and said something along the lines of, 'Hey, this mobile thing is going to blow up — it's going to be important to you — you should have a look and see what we might be able to help you with . . .'

I showed him some of the things we could achieve together to make sure the Garth Brooks brand was represented and doing well on the millions of mobile devices about to become connected multimedia and music players in every American's pocket. From there we continued to work with his team for months to develop a vision of what Garth Brooks, country music legend, should do with the future of mobile entertainment. The next time we met, I was on the end of a bear hug too. Throughout the entire meeting he had his wife and fellow country star Trisha Yearwood chirping across the speakerphone on his mobile, like a walkie-talkie, stepping him through the final stages of a plane she was in that was about to take off. 'Love you too . . .' he'd say. 'I'll call you when I land, honey' we'd hear squawking from the phone resting on the table.

It was surreal. I'd never met a real-deal star before and I'd started with one of the biggest. At first and for years after, I had no idea what to expect of these icons of culture — to an outsider, they are illusory caricatures and media-driven figments of themselves. But now I know for the most part to expect nothing overwhelming. For the most part, they're just human beings, with the same insecurities, the same passions for their families and their friends; they are good at some things and terrible at others and when they want guidance they look for advice. Whatever you do, whatever you know, if you seek to become the best in the world at what that is, then no matter what room you put yourself in, with whichever people, from whatever walks of life, with inner confidence and outer humility, you will hold your own.

Customers were knocking on our door. If you get there first (as we did), and you help create an industry (as we did), then as long as you are good, you become the de facto expert and world thought leadership is *yours to lose*.

If you are among the first to explore and lay at least partial claim to an idea, as long as you get there before there are too many other punters around to make up the rules, *you get to make them up yourself.*

So when people ask me what is the fastest, most sure-fire way to become a thought leader, to be renowned for something and to be an 'expert', I say the secret, which I'll share with you here, is to create or be a part of something totally new. If something is new, there are by default *no* experts, which levels the playing field and equalises the price to pay to become a thought leader down to the person who has the most thoughtful things to say and can share them most creatively. If you embark on a new industry or a new idea then you can help create the new benchmark; if you succeed and can tell a story, everybody points to you as the spokesperson for that revolution.

We continued to set the global benchmark for how to use mobile as an interactive channel for more than talking on the phone. Just before Christmas 2006, we sent the entire office from Auckland to Los Angeles to celebrate a global awards dinner where we picked up five of the 12 awards handed out. In 2007, we made the cover of the leading industry magazine *Adweek*. A campaign we did with David Beckham and Motorola had travelled the world and become so famous it was named the Big Idea of the Year for 2008 by *Brandweek*. We dominated the Oscars of the internet, the Webbies, where we won so many awards that we came second in the Agency of the Year category — losing to R/GA, one of the most famous companies in the industry with over 1000 staff and 30 years of history.

The work continued to tumble in and the recognition continued to flow. We became the most awarded company in the industry for helping the world's most well-known brands use

Whoever gets there first makes the rules.

mobile devices to connect with their consumers. We were living the dream. The world's best. Innovating and creating the future of how people would connect with the world. A future that was starting to come true — it was *real*. It wasn't just that we were doing it, and that people said it couldn't be done — it was that what we'd been saying all along to deaf ears and chuckles in the corner was finally taking over the world. The iPhone arrived in 2007 and in a flash the world began to understand what we had been preaching about since the turn of the century — that this device was destined to change the way people did *everything*.

We were on a roll. Everybody wanted to work for us. Everybody wanted to work *with* us. Everything was going to the right and up. We had become the authorities for the hottest disruption in media and advertising since the internet began, in no small way due to the fact that in many people's eyes we had invented the art and science of *doing it well*, and the heart and nuance of knowing which stories to tell. If there was one thing we became very good at it, it was telling a story. I always painted a vision of what the future looked like in a world of ubiquitous wireless connectivity for all the most well-known brands in society. We became master storytellers with our rusted tin pipe playing the tunes at the vanguard of a movement.

We raised still more money and scaled the business up so hard and fast that the burn rate — what we were investing (and losing) as we blindly chased the God of Growth — was $300,000, $400,000, and sometimes $500,000 a month. Confident. Bold. We believed that outspending our competitors to establish beachheads across the country, to deploy our people in all the key cities, to get our brand everywhere and develop all sorts of innovative technologies and ideas, would see us as the ultimate victor in a highly sought-after market that continued to soar on the upward trajectory we had been experiencing since 2006. With the pressure to move quick and the race to victory in full swing, money started to get loose. The more money you have and the faster the market is growing, the more room you have to make mistakes but the more you can hide your seams too — success and too much resource breed complacency, letting you patch over failures and weaknesses. Still, despite any collateral damage, we were heading in the right direction.

We caught up regularly with Grant Baker, our lead investor, but I remember one of those meetings above all of them like it was yesterday. I can't recall any of the words — it wouldn't be honest to try and repeat them here — I can only remember how I felt leaving. I remember getting the message as clear as day, that Grant's number-one motivation was to build up the company and sell it to make as large a return as possible, whereas my number-one motivation was to create an amazing journey that people wanted to work for, that's known around the world as being the best in the world at what it does, sets a benchmark for Kiwi entrepreneurs and creates the future every day. Who knows, if we do a great job at that maybe we may never sell?

I wondered if Grant doubted my motives a little and that we weren't fully aligned. I never thought that then, but why do I remember this conversation above all others? I wonder if he thought I'd tricked him. I didn't think we were aiming for two different things — I thought that by *wanting* to be the best in the world, and doing what you love best, you would create the most value for your stakeholders because they'd bought into your dream. I thought that *wanting* to create an amazing place to work and to innovate and invent the future would only be good for your brand. But I guess I could be wrong, because you can do all those things and still not make that much money if that's what you prefer to do.

Was I confused? I'd never thought about it. To me, you couldn't do one without the other, or it wouldn't be true. Granted, there was no real purpose to The Hyperfactory; there was no higher cause, other than creating fun jobs and breaking new ground in tech. But still, it had *that* as a purpose, not just money. People wouldn't have stayed if that was all we were there for.

Despite all this, at the height of the American summer of 2008, nothing could possibly stop us. We were unbeatable. Nothing could get in our way of creating the largest, most famous and most valuable type of company that we were. We could think of nothing that would come between us and the dream we'd cooked up in Auckland seven years before from coming true. Nothing, except perhaps a bank I'd read about in a book called *Liar's Poker*; a book I'd read years ago portraying the ruthless greed of Wall Street in a place called Salomon Brothers. But no, I had the wrong brothers. It was the same ruthless greed but actually it was the Lehman Brothers. That's right, Lehman who?

12

Brink

Earlier that February I turned 30. Since the age of 21, I had always envisioned the most spectacular thirtieth birthday party, lasting 30 days and flying 30 friends and family in from around the world in one extended balance of euphoria and recovery. Somehow this idea never quite made it into reality. Instead, in stark contrast to the debauchery of excess and multitudes, as the milestone approached and I had organised nothing, Maya lovingly planned a short escape with just the two of us to nearby Palm Springs. As a Kennedy fan, I knew of Palm Springs only through the episode where Frank Sinatra had invested a huge amount of time and money in preparing his place to host a visit from the young president only to be rebuffed at the very last minute due to pressure surrounding his alleged mob ties. Any place that had Kennedy, mob and Sinatra tied up in it seemed like a cool idea to me.

Palm Springs is in the middle of sparse, sandy Californian desert. We drove a few hours through fields of windmills reaching into the distance until they faded away like tall white flowers across the burned landscape. The Parker had just been done up, set on a 13-acre estate around the original home of a former Hollywood star. It was designed for relaxation and reflection and nothing more. We had massages; sat by the pool under clear blue skies that stretched out to Venus, enveloped in the lukewarm February air; ate good food; did nothing.

That Moleskine in Paris from 2003 started a habit that I would continue forever. I've racked up 10 of them: nine black and one red, stacked up in a pile across five years of time. They weren't special enough any more though, and as I figured they were recording my destiny, I went looking for something better. I found it in Smythson of Bond Street. The Queen uses it, Grace Kelly used it, there's destiny right there.

Each journal comes with 300 featherweight baby blue lined sheets, leather bound, my initials and the years the book holds embossed in gold at the bottom right-hand corner of the cover: 'DGH 2008–'. My great-grandchildren might want to hold this, if not read it. The Smythsons house my plans, my dreams, my paths; they contain nothing less than the blueprints to my life.

I brought two fresh pocket-sized Smythsons with me to Palm Springs, one bright lime green, one black. The black one Maya and I used together, to start planning our life as a unit. When I was little I had seen a five-year plan my dad had scribbled and left on his bedside table, crudely folded up, and no more than one or two sheets of A4 ruled paper, with faint blue horizontal lines down the page and the single red margin down the left-hand side. It seemed so insubstantial that it could have been mistaken for scrap — but what counts is that I remember that it existed.

So Maya and I sat by the pool with our beautiful untouched notebook, and talked and talked while I wrote down the ideas of all the things and dreams we wanted from life. It became our compass for continually ensuring that we were going in the same direction and had some exciting challenging goals to achieve *together.*

The slimmer, green notebook was mine alone and became the world of exploration of the things I believed in: my values. Inspired by Benjamin Franklin and his routine of virtues, as much as I was inspired by the Proust Questions and many other books I'd read along the way, I was determined that now, as my thirtieth year drew to a close, I would once and for all write down the entire set of fundamental core beliefs I held in this world.

Palm Springs brought out a clarity of thought that was largely uninterrupted by the usual monkeys chatting in my mind. As much as I loved being with Maya and escaping LA for a few days, it was a mildly but crisply depressing experience. As well as everything appeared to be going, at 30 I faced up to the long-stewing reality that I didn't even really love what I was doing at The Hyperfactory and that perhaps the adrenalin of beating the odds — the idea of proving Frank Sinatra right — was the real octane in the tank fuelling me. I put that feeling to paper in my Moleskine diaries; I wed myself to the idea that I just needed to finish this off, and close this chapter.

I pulled things back a bit, little by little I drew back, updated or scratched out each ambition. Time was starting to pass me by and on each occasion when I'd sat down to do this in the last three or four years, the one thing I could rely on was consistently reflecting on missed targets and falling short of goals. The reality of what I had set as goals and their likely achievement continued to widen and here, at 30, according to my series of black Moleskines and my documented philosophies and plans of 25 and Onwards, and 26, 27 and 28, I was behind schedule on almost every track I'd set. Sure, the tracks aimed a little high but I still expected more of myself.

I tried a new approach and got a little more directional and a lot less specific. I just asked what I wanted in five years. My answer:

Go confidently in the direction of your dreams. Live the life you have imagined.

Henry David Thoreau

'I want to be able to do exactly whatever I want to do, including:

1. Have total financial freedom for the remainder of my life.
2. Have an international lifestyle and presence.
3. Have active, diversified business interests in creative and lifestyle industries.
4. Be a global thought leader in whatever I choose to do.'

Two new ideas arrived on the scene. I wrote somewhere that I wanted to 'solve real world problems'. Not that I knew what that meant, but it was heading in a fresh direction. The second was that I would try a new theme to life — 'to inspire a future generation of entrepreneurial inspirers' — which was a far cry from the goal of a $100 million portfolio of businesses that I'd been using to direct myself so far. Something was changing. I still had a list of goals but over the years they'd morphed — new things were added and others knocked off, but there were some that were like a tea stain on a coffee table and wouldn't budge. Going to space? Working with Richard Branson? At this point, none of those had even so much as a dent in them but I was determined to keep them on the list. I decided there were too many goals, so I trimmed it in order to focus on far fewer but focus far harder. I cleaned house at the conclusion of these first three decades of living, to set a fresh course for the fourth. Priority number one was to finish the job off at The Hyperfactory as all else seemed to spring from there.

In the US it's very common for companies to raise venture capital funding to accelerate growth at an intense, rapid pace. In essence it involves the art of losing vast sums of money as you commit to a plan that has you winning a war worth winning, and backing it to the hilt unflinchingly until for some reason circumstances force you to change your mind or you have come out as a victor. It takes a certain type of courage and a stomach of steel to build businesses this way; to watch the bank balance drop month after month as a part of the plan. They call this planned dropping a 'burn rate' because you have to be OK with the idea akin to taking suitcases of cash and setting them on fire, in front of your own face, family and friends. This VC-style game is one of ruthless risks and outsized rewards; it's a game where the common rule is that for every 10 companies the investors back, they expect just *one* to be spectacular; it's a game where if you are running a company that's a part of it, you do it knowing that you are being backed at just a one in 10 chance of hitting the big time. Of the other nine companies, it's expected that a couple will do OK, a couple will limp along and the rest will die from starvation of funds. Investors in these types of scenarios will pull the plug on your lifeline — cash — if they believe you aren't going to make it.

We had very brave backers. But they were coming in at the very top of a frothy bubble that was about to come crashing down among a whole series of interconnected events that would eventually bring the world to its knees in ways that nobody ever could have imagined. The carnage we were all about to witness was unimaginable and unprecedented in living memory.

As the summer of 2008 started we all began to notice that the revenue pipeline — what we used to forecast our future sales and cash flow — was not filling up as we had predicted in response to our heavy investments and new hires. We quickly looked at what to do to fix it, brought in outside help, training and moved a few people on. Just six to eight weeks later things were not only looking no better, they were starting to look *worse* as deals that we had forecast as certain to close started vanishing.

What had become a few hundred thousand dollars per month burn rate quickly started to creep towards a half a million dollars and the board, investors and all of us began to get nervous.

On 15 September, those brothers Lehman — one of the most famous investment banks in the world — collapsed. Without an ounce of grace or a minute to breathe, Lehman Brothers collapsed in a way you might imagine a planet from a science-fiction movie to implode in on itself — so quickly and so assuredly as to leave no doubt whatsoever that what once stood tall and propped up a thousand outsized egos was nothing a mere 24 hours later. And the American government stood by and let it happen. Something major was up. Bank after bank began to fall, and what we know now as the global financial crisis started to spiral out of control.

From our Beverly Hills office a few of the team and I would go across the road for a coffee at McCormick & Schmick's, which bizarrely was owned by William McCormick, the United States Ambassador to New Zealand. I would watch the television screens behind the bar and see the New York Stock Exchange Dow Jones index tumble 700 points in a single day. I didn't even own any stocks but I knew this was not about the stocks; it was about confidence in the American economy, which meant confidence in the world economy, which meant all of our clients being confident in their own businesses, which meant me being confident in my business, and all our 150 people around the world.

Sometime within this darkening period I went to visit the internet giant Yahoo to show them some new technology. When I arrived in Sunnyvale, California, the mood was morbid; the Yahoo campus felt like a morgue and I soon realised that the entire company was midway through the process of handing out

5000 pink slips that afternoon. In the US a pink slip is what you get when you've lost your job. You get a pink slip and a cardboard box and are expected to leave by the end of the day. This was happening all over the world in tech, media and beyond and in ways that made Yahoo's lay-offs look like a rounding error — by the end of 2008 Citibank had let 70,000 people go, Hewlett Packard 25,000 and Starbucks 12,000. For the first time in our generation, if you lost your job there was genuine fear about where and when you might get another one.

Meanwhile, like a deer in headlights we were moving embarrassingly slow in the swirl of dangerous events unfolding around us. We held emergency board meetings and in October decided we needed to do a round of redundancies to reduce our burn. That was one of the most painful things I'd ever had to do but in the aftermath of what followed it's now just a blur and I can hardly remember it.

As the next few weeks unfolded, things went from worse to devastating and client after client started pulling their projects; hundreds of thousands of dollars of work just disappeared overnight; every time we updated the pipeline it was thinner and thinner. When a major storm is on its way, the civil defence authorities tell you to stock up on water, canned goods and supplies that you'll need to survive weeks without power or water. You fill up a cupboard with everything you might need: baked beans and batteries, torches and toilet paper, litres upon litres of filtered water, packets and packets of crackers. Our pipeline was our cupboard, and as the storm got worse and worse, it just got emptier and emptier until the barren state of it would see the entire operation out of cash, out of breath and out of business by the end of January 2009. Roughly eight weeks, give or take.

I couldn't believe it.

I'd visited this dark place before.

I'd been here *twice* in fact.

Once with the Fletcher Forests shares when I was young and stupid; and once with Feverpitch, also when I was young and stupid. I thought I knew the meaning of this darkness and mental brutality and that I would never allow myself to risk so much to be here again.

How — *just how* — could I forget to not be so stupid?

The business had its flaws, yes, but it was in crisis largely because the world was in crisis; and because the business was largely my life, my life was in crisis. I resented the world for forcing this upon us. Nobody knew what was happening and where it would stop. How could we be so sure that it wasn't just a blip? Perhaps things would turn around after the New Year. How could we be sure it wasn't going to be 1929 all over again with years of Depression to follow? I know we all know now, but I'm telling you, we didn't know then — nobody did.

I realised we'd made a huge mistake in October. *That* was when I should have taken the knife and cut to the bone, making every single person who wasn't absolutely essential to the future of the business redundant immediately. But *you* try that and see how it feels?

When you look upon all that you've built over almost your entire adult life with your friends and your family, which just months before was going so damn well and you were on the top of the world, and everybody from David Beckham to Garth Brooks was high-fiving you, it is physically and mentally excruciating to think of dismantling it. It's unthinkable to believe that retreat is the only option.

We worked the spreadsheets and numbers to see what we

needed to keep us alive in this corner we'd screwed ourselves into. With each day that passed, the screw tightened and so did the corner — becoming smaller, darker and more constricting by the hour until it was within danger of collapsing in on itself and destroying everything. What should have been one single, deep, devastating head-count cut that left the remaining troops with resolve and the heart to move on with confidence became two jolted cuts that further weakened their roots and heightened their paranoia.

What is this really about? It's about what to do when you have to do really difficult things. Some of the most difficult decisions in life are a series of plasters. How do you pull off a plaster? All at once and with such deliberation as to leave no doubt as to where the plaster is going and who is ripping it off. When you are challenged to make the *really* tough choices in life, family, business — with others, or with yourself — what's most important is to have the *courage* to make those choices so cleanly and decisively, to cut them right through to the bone, to the core of the problem, the core of the opportunity.

Don't half-heartedly decide on anything. Think things through beyond the next move — think two, three, four moves ahead and make decisions based on those possible outcomes instead of just the next, or you'll always be playing catch-up. By the time you've figured out what to do after one move ahead, it can very often be too late. Take some time — imagine all the angles, and imagine all the possible ways to create the future; but once you've weighed it all up, and once you've picked a path, commit with your whole heart and all your energy.

The bloodshed of the next round of redundancies is tattooed on the inside of my mind. I was in the apartment in Santa Monica overlooking the ocean; it was a dark evening the week before Christmas and we had an ominous call with the management team to decide whether to make the second round of cuts before the holidays or after. This wasn't a normal redundancy — if you lost your job now, along with tens of thousands of people every week, you were really staring into a long winter of hibernation, no matter how incredible you were. So our choices were, tell people they are screwed before Christmas, or tell them they are screwed after Christmas.

I laid out the pros and cons and shared my vote.

'If it were me. I'd want to know now. None of this BS of "Happy Holidays" when we know damn well the day they get back they're fired. Tell them the truth as soon as we have decided. Tell them now that they have no job after Christmas.'

I argued for before because it would save us two weeks of payroll cash — a huge amount in the context of our dwindling supply — and at least then the affected staff weren't being deceived that they had a job to return to in the New Year. It was my decision, but we went around one by one on the call for the others to share what they thought.

'After.'

'After.'

'After.'

'After.'

'After.'

Each of them — other than Jeff Arbour — argued for after Christmas because they believed that in these frightening times where every family across the country was worried about keeping their jobs, we should allow them to have as comfortable and enjoyable a Christmas as possible, and deal the news out in January when everybody returned. Jeff is an entrepreneur more than he is an employee, which is why he voted the way he did.

Half a decision is no decision at all.

We hung up.

I agonised, knowing that every dollar of cash we saved would give us a few more weeks to survive and that my focus should be on the morale of the remaining staff, not the ones we were letting go. I was also aware that how we handled the departures would affect what all those who were left thought of us. For this special situation where I couldn't trust what my gut was telling me, against my own judgment, I leant on the counsel of the rest of the team who seemed unanimous on a January timeline.

After the phone went down, I cried.

It was a cleansing cry as I came to the realisation that perhaps once again, I was about to lose it all. I wasn't angry, I wasn't forlorn. I didn't blame anybody or myself but I did feel very alone, even with Maya right beside me. I just knew that I had to *really* start getting used to the fact that as the leader, I was largely responsible for losing what my family and I had spent almost a decade building. I had tried to 'go big' — for the *second* time — but it looked like I was going home instead: empty-handed. Sure, at 30 I was still young, but maybe I wasn't cut out to do this entrepreneur thing? Maybe I should just go back to New Zealand and get a job. Maybe I should try to live a normal, easier life, under the radar, sticking to the straight and narrow and trying *possible* things?

I hadn't given up. In the morning and each and every day that we still had life in us — that is, every day that we still had cash left in the bank — I had to work on three possible eventualities in parallel. Plan A (and by far my preferred choice) was to summon from the gods (any and all of them) the grit, the determination and the answers to work our way out of this hole, as much as it was looking increasingly impossible. It meant convincing the organisation that remained that we *could* make it through so they didn't start jumping ship; it meant raising new capital, cutting costs and driving sales — and it meant doing *all* of those things at the same time, and in a matter of weeks.

Plan B (and by far my least preferred option) was to work with our existing investors to recapitalise the company and start again, which meant getting rid of most of the staff and heavily diluting a lot of the earlier backers. Already exhausted from the last five-year sprint and losing passion for what we'd started, I thought I would rather start something else entirely and just walk away for a clean break than do that if it came to it. Out of all the plans, Plan C ended up being *the* plan with the most profound impact on my life in that moment and forever after; the plan of all plans, the one plan that every single one of us needs to create one day, for our one life, on this one planet. But this is not the right place to tell you about it. Let's start with Plan A.

13

Plan A

Plan A.

    Rabbits out of hats.

    Houdini's chains.

    Maradona's 'Hand of God'.

    James Bond's escapes.

    This was the realm which we were now in.

    Let's start by mapping out as many different theoretical routes through the barriers of all probability. Let's be as prepared to have to make every single one of them come right at the same time as we are to expect any single one of them to fail us.

    With Plan A we had sketched out an entire list of possible scenarios or escape routes; looking back in the Moleskine diary that shows the days and weeks of this period unfolding, the list included: shut the New Zealand office; shut Asia; shut Australia; shut subsidiary brands we had just set up; raise debt finance; do a joint venture with company Z; approach company Y for a lifeline; find a knight to ride in on a white horse and save us; and the last one on the list, 'do whatever it takes to get to a break-even position immediately'. We were simultaneously keeping all wires live and pursuing all live wires.

    The most sensible thing to do for Plan A to have a chance was to try to get ourselves under our own control and reduce our losses.

Grant me the serenity to accept the things I cannot change, the courage to change the things I can, and the wisdom to know the difference.

Reinhold Niebuhr

Facing pending disaster or intense stress, identify what you can and can't control. Letting go of the things you can't control gives you the peace of mind to focus intently on the things that you can.

We had some clients that remained solid and who had told us they were committed to seeing us through without pulling out, so we needed to deliver on those projects; delivering was within our control. We had expenses and an overhead that we had built; cutting or reducing budgets were two levers that were entirely within our own control. We could push as hard as we possibly could to get more sales in an environment where the buyers who weren't already themselves fired had frozen their wallets. But that was out of our control.

We needed to bring the expenses down far enough in line to match the amount of cash coming in from the clients we could rely on. We had to get the damn burn rate to a place that was manageable, a level where we might need to raise just a few hundred thousand dollars (versus a few million) to cushion us to safely course correct and slide back into profitability. I believed we *could* raise more money and of course we'd already started to try but that was still in the 'out of our control' bucket, so priority number one was to get our cash burn down and dismantle this global machine even faster than we'd built it. How much time did we have? About 60 days.

When things come to a crunch, extricate and elevate yourself from the moment. Somewhere far above, safe and silent, where you can see all the moving parts and buy yourself just a little of whatever it is that you need to keep going. The general shorthand for this is *time*. Nobody is getting any more time. Not you, not me. *We have the time that we have* — it doesn't stretch or shrink, it is what it is and it's the only thing that equalises us all. Beneath the notion of *time* it is actually something *else* that you really need. Sometimes that's strength — you need to catch your breath, remind yourself of who you are and where you've been to refill your pool of confidence and inner fortitude; sometimes it's opinions — you need to canvas a few trusted sources and a few ideas from a few unexpected quarters to see a few fresh angles; sometimes it's sleep, to re-energise your mind and body. Whatever it is, it's never *just* time, it's the thing that time *buys* you that you are after.

For businesses, when we say we need more time, what time equates to is always money. A business doesn't stop if you close the door tonight — the power, premises and people still need to get paid tomorrow. Unlike a lot of things in life, you can't just put a business on the backburner for a few days or weeks. It burns all right, but not the type of backburner you might want. More specifically, time in a high-growth, scaling enterprise often means readily available cash that you could go down to the bank and pull out this afternoon. Cash flow is the lifeblood of freedom and flexibility for a venture, and an entrepreneur — and the *lack* of it is the killer of a thousand incredible companies nobody could imagine disappearing, the nail in the foreclosure of a million mortgages.

It's often not a lack of assets or a lack of wealth that brings people down, but a lack of cash to keep feeding the machine while you restructure your affairs to shore things up and move a few bits and pieces around. In a start-up venture, the cash runway is your stamina monitor and dictates the range of options that you can consider. If you have a runway of 24 months, you can truly think strategically and make difficult decisions that you might not be able to if you have only eight weeks before you'll be forced into positions you otherwise might not take. As a rule of thumb today in a high-growth technology

No pressure, no diamonds.

Thomas Carlyle

start-up, if you have 12 months' cash flow it's sufficient, 18 is great and 24 ideal. But, 60 days?

Earlier in the year we had raised another round of financing solely to scale the business in what was to be the most aggressive expansion phase the company had ever had. We were putting more and more chips on the table just as things around the world were getting worse and worse — unknown to us — because we were focused on the task at hand and not the world at large. We were doing the exact *opposite* of what we should have been doing. When Lehman Brothers imploded and the clients dried up and the cash runway shrank, I had pictures of an F1 cockpit view speeding down an ever-shortening straight towards a brick wall. The cuts we made in early January were like a brave attempt to take that car from roaring along in top speed and suddenly throw it into reverse, with slim chance and very little room for error. Like so many things before, it seemed impossible and — as much as that was what our DNA told us always to overcome — this time, given the fear around the world, given that lifelines were nowhere to be seen, I realised that perhaps just this once, we were pushing our luck a tiny bit too far to expect fate and fortune to come to the party.

I tried to invite them anyway. In one painful week in January 2009 we pulled all sorts of triggers on Plan A to salvage a future. Offices were shut and people were laid off in all time zones. Los Angeles, Chicago, San Francisco, Sydney were all folded; Auckland and Hong Kong downsized; the remaining core of the US team (including me) shipped off to New York and hunkered down to ride this out as a unit. We let go dozens and dozens of people and many of the early team members and the entire Indian office of 50 people took big pay cuts to help us get through. We started to see our way out of a deep dark hole. I wasn't asking anybody to do anything I wasn't prepared to do myself. I wanted as much as possible to create a quilt of mutuality — that we share the pains in order to be able to see through to the gains, whatever they may be. Geoffrey and I stopped taking a salary and I personally handled the meetings with many of the people who lost their jobs. Sadly I became very good at it, although that doesn't make it that much easier.

Wading through the fog of uncertainty we could barely see past the next 30 days; I was struggling to visualise how we'd salvage anything to make it through a continual series of extreme, seemingly unending challenges. There is a saying that probably has its origins centuries ago — *what would Jesus do?* Popular-culture pundits of technology, business, art and design have hijacked that to become *what would (Steve) Jobs do?* I hijack it further and expand it to carousel through an entire suite of figures that I've pulled together since Napoleon Hill coerced me to list them in Paris in 2003. In opportunity as much as in crisis I always look to them for inspiration: heroes of history, of politics, creativity, adventure, war, social change. I dive deep into everything I know and have learned of and from them, and I draw on what they might counsel or do. For some reason, as the pressure of Christmas 2008 built to a crescendo, I looked to another Napoleon — Bonaparte, this time — who time after time got himself out of the most impossible scrapes.

A simple Corsican cadet who became self-appointed Emperor of France and King of Italy by the time he was 34, he faced a ruthless series of challenges in his unlikely rise to Continental domination. He commanded absolute loyalty from his troops and generals and had vision far beyond his contemporaries, the scale of which was to be his undoing when

When you get into a tight place and it seems you can't go on, hold on, for that's just the place and the time that the tide will turn.

Harriet Beecher Stowe

he attempted to take Russia — always a bad idea. By March 1814 he was under attack by the Allied forces of almost a quarter of a million to his 70,000; despite this, in a campaign weeks earlier his 30,000 defeated the Prusso-Russian Allies' 120,000 in north-eastern France. Similar stories abound of him repeatedly defeating the odds. But time always catches up with a man tempting his chances and this time arrived in the form of the Duke of Wellington, who bore down and steadily pushed him back until his defences collapsed in on themselves, allowing the Allies to march upon Paris on 30 March 1814. Napoleon was captured and forced to abdicate the throne.

On a series of grim evenings, after the dark had settled in and I escaped from the issues at hand, I searched the internet for stores in Paris that sold letters Napoleon had written. I flipped through and translated them one by one as they spoke prosaically of moving troops from here to there, of resupplying barracks or horses, of accounts of treasury and taxes before I stumbled across one, handwritten and addressed to his Minister of War. It was dated March 1814. I knew from the timing that it was just days before the surrender to Wellington — by this stage all reasonable hope of him making it through was gone, but from the tone of the letter you sure as hell couldn't tell it.

The 200-year-old words spoke to me. First, as an ephemeral reminder of the scale of ambitions of young leaders in times past; which always makes me feel very small and reminds me to dream very big. At the same time, it's a stinging testament to the fact that confidence easily turns into arrogance, avarice and lack of focus; Napoleon's ill-prepared and overstretched *grand armée* was now strewn across the entire continent from the Portuguese peninsula to Moscow. Lastly, its obvious main thrust — to lead from the front, double down to the very end, knowingly on the verge of capitulation — is that of a leader's undying and even *unreasonable* commitment to his vision even where sense says it might be time to call it a day.

Once I'd found it, I knew that it would be my talisman to get me through; I promised myself that *when* we got out of this mess — in whatever form — I would buy the text as soon as I could afford to as a token of what it felt like to stare at the absolute loss of everything but make it through the other side.

> Letter signed 'NP' addressed to Clark, Duke of Feltre, Minister of War. La Ferte-sous-Jarre, 2 March 1814:

> Write to the Duke of Dalmatia and tell him, with the troops that he has, he must and can defeat the enemy if he shows audacity and leads from the front. He should know that we are in a time where one needs double the resolution and double the vigour of ordinary times. If he manoeuvres with alacrity and leads by example as the first to put himself in danger, he must with the troops that he has, defeat double of his enemy.

> NP

14

Wiry

Four or five months before this catastrophe was unfolding, I walked into a nondescript and faded building in Chelsea, New York, and strode up the stairs behind a beautiful, tall young girl who stopped halfway up to change out of her Vans sneakers and into her high heels. Under her arm she was holding a large folio that all models in New York carry like a billboard. We left the stairs on the same floor and I walked down the corridors looking for Madison Alley Capital. There were no signs anywhere, so I walked my way backwards and opened the first door that seemed like there might be people behind it, only to look straight at the very same girl surrounded by four or five equally stunning and tall Eastern Europeans; she gave me a small smile.

'Madison Alley Capital?'

If only — they would have been the best-looking bankers in the world. But no, the modelling agency had never heard of their supposed neighbours. Bad sign. I continued my walk through the corridor and finally came to the room where Michael Seidler greeted me. I stepped into a space of about 30 square metres. There was a desk in one corner and another small glass table in another; on it fresh fruit — pineapples, strawberries and melon — was laid out on a paper plate. I was offered coffee and soft drinks in plastic cups. There was no other furniture and no windows. *This* was Madison Alley Capital, and this operation was supposed to help me raise $10 million.

Before the clouds started forming, at the start of the summer I had spent a few weeks contacting and interviewing bankers who wanted to help The Hyperfactory raise new capital. Michael was the last in a long list. He was a wiry, small, quiet Jewish chap, and was busy fussing over a BlackBerry phone scrappily hooked up to a small crackly speaker that looked like it was bought in Chinatown — he was trying to create a makeshift conference phone in order to call our investor Grant back in New Zealand, who was helping me select the banker. All the others I had visited had offices on very high floors, large spacious conference rooms with ground-to-ceiling views of Manhattan and beyond. They offered piping-hot coffee and herbal teas in fine china, demure receptionists and no less than four sharply dressed partners to talk about how they would make my dreams come true.

After all the interviews and proposals submitted by the good and the great of boutique bankers in New York City who wanted our business, you can guess who we chose: the scrappy start-up, the battler. The logic? As Grant impressed on me, Michael working for us would mean a *lot* more to Michael than it would to any other firm we could have picked, and we were confident he knew every bit as much as the others did, he just had less manpower and flash to show for it. If we became Michael's client, he *needed* to make this work because as one person he could only take on a few clients, and in banking, if you don't get deals done, you don't eat. Michael needed to eat.

We initially contracted Michael during the frothy times to help us raise $10 million to scale the business even further, and we went to visit all the largest companies in the world, from Microsoft to Time Warner, who might have had an interest in being a part of our journey. One by one, presentation after presentation, the level of interest was gauged but once Lehman Brothers fell, all bets were off. Nobody was buying or investing in anything; everybody was just focusing on survival and laying off their own staff. Everybody but Meredith.

Every time we met, Michael and I would go through a list with all the shit-hot names of possible investors and one day he added another one that to me at least was less shit hot than most: *Meredith*.

'Meredith who?'

'They're in Des Moines, Iowa,' Michael replied.

'Des Moines, where?'

As it turns out, Iowa is in the middle of America. They have an annual state fair and in 2011 for its centenary the state celebrated by debuting a new treat of a deep-fried block of butter on a stick. Meredith is a publishing giant that was started almost 110 years ago by the Meredith family and has grown to dominate the American women's mass-media market with titles such as *Better Homes and Gardens*, one of the largest magazines in circulation in the world. They are similar to other big magazine and media companies such as Condé Nast or Hearst, but it is a company called Scripps that is one of their biggest competitors. Scripps just happened to be one of our biggest clients. They own the Food Network and dozens of other properties targeted at the American mum and we were doing a lot of work for them. More interesting to us than all of this was that the Meredith Corporation from Des Moines, Iowa, was starting to invest and buy up companies like ours to help their advertisers understand new media — the internet, search engines, Facebook — things like that. Next on their list was a company that was a leader at understanding mobile, and up there for consideration was The Hyperfactory.

As I continued to work my way through Plans A, B and C, I focused furiously on getting under our own control and whatever else happened, happened. Around the same time in December that we were running through the slash and burn we were going to inflict on the entire global operation, a three-person team from Meredith came to visit us at the offices in Beverly Hills. It was all very relaxed and I was open with them that we were seeing a lot of drop-off in clients and general paralysis in the marketplace, which they understood and didn't seem too worried about. I was equally upbeat about many clients who were looking incredibly promising before the financial meltdown had hit us all.

I did my homework and prepped hard with the help of Michael; I thought through every angle as to what I might do to leave a dent and then stepped back to let everything relax and wash over me. I decided the right approach was just to take it as it came.

My preference in general is always to be unassuming, quiet and calm. And patient. I try to talk less than the other guy and ask a few questions towards the end. I am not a hand-waving, exuberant and extroverted convincer. I attempt to convince people in a slow, steady way; I might pose a problem or a vision, and then paint a picture piece by piece leading up to an inevitable conclusion — a conclusion that I like to leave the other side to make for themselves in their own time, but if I have to I'll force it.

Everybody has a different style; I'd tried out a few and this is what suits me best. I was composed, living in every minute with the opposing reality that the business was on a knife's edge to survive so we really could do with a 'white knight' like Meredith now more than ever; but equally our history and everything we had built up over the years still made ours the most sought-after brand in the industry. We were just about the last independent company that hadn't been sold that still had some scale. To the right investor we would be worth a premium.

What I needed to pull off the impossible just one more time was a quiet, deeply stilled confidence in the long view, and the courage to shed all visible signs of the short-view struggles that greeted us every day in the office to face a crumbling little empire that had 60 days to live. In fact that confidence and calmness was what I needed *every* day just to show up to the troops — a leader, Napoleon said, is a dealer in hope. You can't deal in hope if you don't harbour any yourself.

Later that evening we were to go out to dinner in Santa Monica, not far from where I lived. I'd heard about these kinds of dinners before, the kind where big deals start and finish, and I felt another fork coming towards me. For an important dinner, I don't remember much about the place. I think it had Arizonian orange stucco walls and a muted brown carpet with understated waiters in little penguin suits, but I could be entirely wrong.

John and Wendy from Meredith began telling me the company story and to softly sell themselves as a really great fit for us. John invested in the companies and Wendy ran them. They talked about how well previous deals had gone and how Meredith is a steady, stable company that makes decisions for the long haul, and that they needed this transaction to become a leader in mobile.

We ordered a bottle of nice red from Frank Family Vineyards, the vineyard of our investor, Rich Frank. And as we began to drink, I decided I really liked these guys. They got what we did and what we wanted to be and they were very right

A leader is a dealer in hope.

Napoleon

about the fit. The Hyperfactory made its name doing flashy, innovative and ground-breaking work for many of the sexiest brands in the world, like Coke, Motorola and Nike. Although we'd done jobs here and there for the mainstream brands that served what is known as 'middle America', we were struggling to be taken seriously for seven-figure deals — too 'creative, too edgy and flighty' — not solid, reliable and dependable enough. Meredith was nothing if not reliable and dependable. They were the primary provider of knowledge and content for the American woman and household for over a century — maybe even a little staid. Meredith would have given us the credibility to convince mass-market brands like Kraft and Nestlé at scale, and we would have given Meredith the credibility to be cool and ahead of the curve on the most important new new thing.

In my only conscious tactical decision, towards the end of the dinner I dropped in how well our relationship with Scripps was going and as we left John tossed out that I might want to take a trip on the Meredith private jet.

It often isn't what you say, but what is left unsaid, that lingers long after the conversation is over. People are always in a rush to say directly what they mean; blind to the idea that there are 10 different ways to say something without actually saying it. I planted the seed that perhaps their rival was circling to take a stake in us so they might want to shuffle things along, while John threw out a bone that perhaps I should head to Iowa to meet the chief executive in order to do just that.

The team from Meredith ended up being one of the most straight-shooting group of people I'd met in business. Discussions progressed in only one direction: forward. What they said, they meant; no politics and no dirty tricks. But something did turn up that really took me by surprise — as things moved forward they made it very clear that they actually had no interest in investing new capital in the business. *All* we were after was new capital — we needed it to shore us up, and to push through the difficult times that were bound to lie in the year ahead. If they didn't want to inject new capital, what did they want? As it turns out, they only wanted one thing — to *buy* us — and as it happens I was quietly fascinated by the idea of taking a trip on a private jet.

I'd never flown private before. I'd heard all about it and I'd seen the Learjets lined up at airports all over the world but had no idea what it was like getting on one; not having to walk through torturous and dehumanising airport security; not having a schedule or a gate to be at; being able to turn around and go wherever you want with just a nod to the captain.

A large black Cadillac Escalade SUV four-wheel drive pulled in to pick me up and off we headed to Teterboro airport in New Jersey, where you will only ever find private planes. I walked across the tarmac, up the few stairs, and settled into a roomy tan leather seat. In about the same amount of time it would have taken me to get to the commercial airport, check in and go through security to wait to board, we had landed in Des Moines for a Meredith board meeting that I was to present at later in the day. I returned to New York, we'd continue phone calls, they'd ask for things and I'd send them over; we met more of their people, they met more of ours. Days and weeks went by and all I was waiting for was an email with an offer.

We kept working relentlessly to get things under our own control when one day early in the New Year that email finally landed in my inbox. It looked too simple. A badly designed PowerPoint document outlined the key terms of the deal between us in 10 slides. Meredith would buy 19.9 per cent of the company immediately for what equated at the time to just under eight figures in New Zealand dollars — and they would have an exclusive option to buy the rest within two years at a full price ultimately dependent on our financial performance. Ten slides. Almost ten million dollars. So close, but we weren't yet there. We had a *lot* of work still to do.

In the background, switching from the bigger picture to the immediate pressures of the day, with the draft deal in hand, we got to work securing some bridging finance to give us the room we needed to breathe until we got ourselves operating at break even. They call it that because it bridges you over the deep shit to the other end where you expect to climb out of it. Michael lined up a bank that was willing to lend us money based on what our clients owed us. As we sent clients an invoice, even though they hadn't yet paid up (and by the time they did so, we could have been dead), the bank would lend us *today* up to around 70 per cent of what we were owed. It brought in a few hundred thousand dollars in cash overnight. Next, he found us some private bridge lenders — gutsy people who take a bet on a situation where they know a person or company is in a tight spot, but there is a strong chance of them coming through. They loan you a chunk of money on a short term, secured against the assets of the business at a high interest rate *plus* a bonus fee if the event you are counting on comes through. This brought in another few hundred thousand dollars. Thanks to Magic Michael, we had a new injection of about half a million in cash — a lifeline of inches, but inches we desperately needed.

In *Any Given Sunday*, the character Tony D'Amato (played by Al Pacino) preaches about inches and he's right — life *is* about inches. The inches fate takes away from you, and the inches you take from fate. These inches between failure and success are the

Life is just a game of inches.

inches that make you, you. These are the inches that test you. These are the inches that make life worth living. I've been either side of inches, and I've had them work for me and work against me. Here we were again, just inches away from the finish line, but that meant the finish line was still precious inches away from us — and in this game, at this time, in this state of affairs that the world found itself in — *anything* could happen.

15

Leaving

According to Wikipedia, in American football a Hail Mary is an unimaginably long forward pass made in desperation with only a small chance of success, especially at or near the end of a half. Wiry little Michael had thrown one. The seconds closed down on the clock and our hearts were in our mouths as the ball spiralled through the air.

Brinksmanship was a dangerous game to chance but with the bridge loans buying us a few more days of survival, I nudged back a handful of red-line changes for a marginally better deal, more to make it appear as if we were equals than anything else. Agreeing on the spot to the first thing we opened would have shown another poor card in our hand and would fill the room with a mustardy cloud of weakness. It worked. Things moved along and we got ever closer, in better and better shape.

As the ball spiralled up towards the clouds, we saw eye to eye, signed a term sheet of deal points to sell The Hyperfactory Limited, of Auckland, New Zealand, to the Meredith Corporation, of Des Moines, Iowa. We'd agreed a grace period to allow Meredith to check out the facts and get to know us better, and if they decided they didn't like anything so much as the colour of my socks, they could pretty much pull out. We would all aim to settle the deal on 1 July 2009 and just like they do in the movies, the lawyers filed in immediately to turn those points we'd shaken hands on into a long-form contract that they would argue over, line by line, for the longest hundred days of my life while I waited for Michael's ball to come back down to earth and for the grace period to run out.

Days after that signing, on 14 March 2009, I was standing at the edge of the unspoiled Whangapoua beach in the Coromandel Peninsula of New Zealand, preparing to get married in just over an hour. We awoke to driving rain from an opaque silver sky that stopped and cleared just as our friends, our family, our team started to arrive to watch us.

Few of them knew Maya was inches from being married to a pauper and a failure. An embarrassment. Few of them knew that together we were inches from having to start a life from scratch like so many newlyweds — building together from a base of nothing but love. Fewer still knew that throughout it all, she hadn't so much as flinched. How embarrassing for her to be marrying somebody who everybody thought was doing *so* well, who only the month before had actually lost it *all*. How devastating for me to start my married life with *nothing* and to have this beautiful, perfect woman who came halfway across the world to support me have to go through us starting all over again, *again*.

Instead here we were, among all our family and friends from across the world, and our future was secured. Things couldn't have looked more different than how they had looked less than a hundred days ago. I had just turned 31.

I love Post-it notes. I use them everywhere — every colour, every size. I can't imagine a world without them. When we returned to America I took out a fresh pad of yellow ones, 5 cm by 3 cm, unwrapped the cellophane and in thick marker wrote down 100, flipped to the next one and wrote 99, flipped to the next one and wrote 98, 97, 96 . . . 5, 4, 3, 2, 1. 100 days. Every morning I pulled one off as I walked out of the apartment, marking one day closer to the beginning of the end of The Hyperfactory. From the very first note, I knew that something had changed. With the signing of the deal, Meredith paid a deposit and with all the work we put into Plan A starting to come right, morale was lifting, revenue was coming back, we were getting very close to being under our own control and the break-even point was near. Even if the deal fell through now, we'd still be standing, I knew that much. We'd weathered the storm. No matter what might end up happening to derail the deal in these 100 days to follow, we'd all pulled together and pulled off Plan A.

But nothing happened. The Post-it notes peeled off one after the other and 1 July rolled around. We announced that we had sold 19.9 per cent of the company to Meredith Corporation, a major international media conglomerate who wanted our little Kiwi start-up. I remember one thing so vividly and clearly above all else that it was seared on my soul — as I was reading the story in the *New Zealand Herald* online from our tiny Tribeca apartment overlooking the Hudson River, there was a peaceful feeling of happiness and an important milestone checked off. As I read down the article towards my quoted closing words, 'It proves young people can do this. That you can build a global business with entrepreneurs from Auckland — I think that is the thing I'm most proud of.' This is where I stopped and broke down while Maya stood looking over my shoulder, bewildered. Crying. For the third time in such a distinctive, memorable way in our now decade-long relationship, but this time because of a complex cocktail of pride, happiness and relief rather than apprehension, hopelessness and regret.

Although the freedom that a small pile of money brought

was liberating, my emotions had very little to do with money; although the adrenalin of creating world firsts year after year was a rush of pride every time, it wasn't that; and although making it from the edge of the world — quite literally as far as you could go — to set up camp and *win* in New York, the very definition of a city of 'success', was so gratifying, it wasn't that; although the ultimate success in business is sometimes building something that somebody else thinks is so worthy that they want to buy it, whole, it wasn't that either. Being a 'successful' business faded into the background; what I was overwhelmed by on that day and in that moment had nothing to do with any of those things.

The feelings that rose within me that afternoon as I read the article had nothing to do with any of those victories and *everything* to do with our story serving to inspire young people everywhere, as just one tiny, small example that you don't *need* to ask for permission to do things older people say 'you can't'; you don't *need* to wait for anybody to go out there and start your dream; you don't *need* to be experienced or qualified or smarter, faster, bigger, better to start a journey and build it into a global mark of brilliance. You just need to believe in *yourself*, believe it can be done and *go and do it*.

That day only confirmed to me what I had thought I had started to discover a few years earlier — that what lit me up the most, and gave me more satisfaction than almost everything, what was my core underlying driver that maybe motivated me beyond all else, was to try and serve as even a small dose of inspiration to others. So, what did that mean? What *was* it then out of this whole journey that I had wanted more than anything? I think I really met my fate, squarely in the eye, in the timeless minute that hung in the air after reading those words in that article: *I wanted to show that this could be done.*

Like many small countries and towns across the globe, New Zealand has a long-standing culture of bringing down and doubting the daring dreams of its people as much as it has a culture of silence in success. It's a twin affliction where one enduringly undermines the other. As long as we continue to laugh and ridicule those who try — no matter how outrageous their attempts — at the same time as those who succeed retreat under the cloak of presumed modesty, the vicious cycle of encouraging dreamers to quit and winners to quieten will leave us void of an achievement and success mentality or inspiration.

On paper our entire story was one word: impossible. In a business plan it would have been laughed out of every boardroom or business school: 22-year-old kids start a company in a tiny country with no venture capital community or tech start-up culture to speak of, perched on the edge of the world dreaming to help start an industry that *didn't* exist; they take it global across seven cities, working in six continents, hiring hundreds of people to reach the very pinnacle of their field only to lead themselves to the threshold of their very own demise in the worst financial crisis since 1929; and just a few months later sell all that they'd built to a 107-year-old New York Stock Exchange-listed giant for millions of dollars. Impossible. But it happened.

The Hyperfactory did well in 2010, made a record profit, grew fast and in July Meredith triggered their option to buy the 80.1 per cent they didn't already own. The New Zealand dollar soared and nobody made what they call 'F-you' money — the type of rich where you can do whatever you want for the rest of your life — but our investors made a return, we did OK and a chapter of our lives was beginning to end.

Within a few short months, the strangest question settled

in: what to do with the money?

I'm not sure why I was at all surprised — we never did anything notable with any spare money we'd had to date anyway, so why all of a sudden should I expect our view on the world to change just because we had a little more? The odd thing is, somewhere in my subconscious I think I *knew* all this already from experiences Maya and I had had. Years before, when we found ourselves every now and then in circumstances of the greatest luxury, I was at first fascinated by the way the uber-rich live. What disturbed me was not the extravagance itself but that the trappings so quickly became all too familiar. They became just one more *level*, and after a few days within them I never felt any better or any worse, rather that I'd just reached a *new* normal that was too easy to get used to. I worried then that if *this* is what happens every time you move up a rung in the improbable stakes of excess and means, then no wonder the world becomes a twisted, desperate, misguided battle of who can have *more*.

We had a little bit more money come in — not a ton, but there was the promise of a lot more. Mostly, we spent the rest of the next year doing little things that we otherwise might not have — I called up that little store in Paris and bought that letter Napoleon wrote — but nothing else really changed. Well, one thing did. I knocked off the first step of one of the things that had been at the top of my list of 'to do's' now for almost 10 years.

I hunted down the local space agent and sat down with her one ordinary afternoon to reserve my seat on one extraordinary spacecraft — the Virgin Galactic SpaceShipTwo. When it's ready, it will take six of us 120,000 metres in the sky at five times the speed of sound, piercing into space. I was about the three-hundredth person in the world to sign up — in the history of the universe only 528 people have ever ventured into space.

Aside from my own childhood fascination, their stories give me no doubt as to why I want to do this. Every single astronaut to return to Earth has claimed a similar thing — that seeing our fragile planet from afar would reinforce your humanity, your compassion and caring for all human beings and living things, including our living world — to an extent that will never leave you. All that we have ever known, in the history of humanity, has happened on the small blue and white marble that I will look down on from space.

I want to see that vulnerability. I want to see the wholeness. I want to be one of those first few hundred human beings in history to see that with my own eyes — and to be able to tell my children and their children that their father and grandfather went up there first, to be a better person. To serve this planet better. To serve our fellow humans better. That is why I want to go.

Shortly after the tenth birthday party for The Hyperfactory, at the end of 2010, I decided that I was going to leave. In April 2011, a new boss who I was to report to arrived at Meredith and over our very first beer in his very first week on the job I resigned with my final day to be the last working day of the year.

No leaving party. No celebration. Not even a goodbye really. After 10 years, one morning in December I walked through the office doors as Derek Handley, CEO, The Hyperfactory and walked out of them that evening as Derek Handley, unemployed.

Look again at that dot. That's here. That's home. That's us. On it everyone you love, everyone you know, everyone you ever heard of, every human being who ever was, lived out their lives. The aggregate of our joy and suffering, thousands of confident religions, ideologies, and economic doctrines, every hunter and forager, every hero and coward, every creator and destroyer of civilisation, every king and peasant, every young couple in love, every mother and father, hopeful child, inventor and explorer, every teacher of morals, every corrupt politician, every 'superstar', every 'supreme leader', every saint and sinner in the history of our species lived there — on a mote of dust suspended in a sunbeam.

Carl Sagan

16

Plan C

So what about Plan C? If Plan A was to claw ourselves out of the mess (which, thankfully, we did), and if Plan B was to restructure the company and essentially start from scratch (which, thankfully, we didn't), what was Plan C? The one that proved to be *the* most important of all — and the hundred days that changed my life forever while it all hung in the balance?

Plan C was simple. Plan C was to do everything I could to mentally prepare for the loss of it all, to paint as vivid a picture as possible of what 'life after' might look like, and to *practise* living, being OK with it to prepare for when it happens. During those dusky evenings of that Christmas and New Year's of 2008 I held a series of meetings with myself, asking the hardest questions I could imagine of the situation, should it come to that. Would I start again, again? Is this what I really want to do with my life? Would we go home? I wanted to become friends with these scenarios, and to know them well before I had to meet them.

The last time I'd screwed up this big it was about 'How do I get right back on the horse and keep going?' This time it was questioning whether the horse was the right thing to be riding in the first place. I usually sleep very soundly, but during these nights I couldn't sleep at all. The monkeys in my head were arguing and chattering amongst themselves. The ulcers in my mouth were building up and the knots in my stomach wouldn't untie themselves for a minute.

I strung up a tightrope of opposing realities to reconcile with my *self* what February or March 2009 would feel like under this looming cloud of fortune, at the same time as resolving not to give in and quit. At one end of the rope, in the daytime I gave it absolutely everything to make Plan A work with a determination that I wouldn't accept anything less and that success and survival was the most important thing in the world, our very livelihoods depending on it; in the evenings at home, I would carefully creep across to the other end, and invest in the spiritual harmony of being at peace with the possible relinquishing of it all, leaning on the crutch of faith that as long as I had health and family, I had a future and none of it really mattered at all.

I couldn't find any other way to deal with the situation that didn't mean on the one hand giving up in weakness, and on the other losing perspective on my good fortune. I couldn't afford to do either — nobody can. That's what makes us human — to strive until the end, but not at the cost of all that is good in our lives or by being blind to the relative misfortune of others.

I'd run through my checklist of behaviours to defeat the demons of difficulty, a list that was getting sharper and better as I was getting stronger and older.

Double down and give it *everything*. Map every possible solution. Tilt all possibilities and probabilities in your favour. Work on what you can control, let go of what you can't. Be inspired through history and greatness. Believe in yourself and deal in hope. *Make your problems bigger.*

When the pressure mounts and the universe keeps piling it on as you crouch to contain it from falling in on you — our shadow side starts to show. This side is how we respond to what life throws at us — how well we know these shadows lets us respond with grace.

I respond by trying to take in as expansive a picture as I can. I float in my mind, high enough above everything to make sense of it all as one interconnected view of the world, to see all the moving parts and meditate on how best to put them together. The more the problems mount, the higher the pressure builds — the higher I want to go. That's where *how do we make this problem bigger* fits in.

As each night drew to a close, I tried to shrink my problems through relativity. In my mind, I unhooked myself from the chains of the daily difficulties, in search of what would *really* matter in five, 10 or 20 years. Here, under this most extreme pressure and needing to see the bigger picture, the universe was really trying to tell me something — she wasn't about to let this crisis go to waste. And I was going to squeeze every drop from it and question *everything*.

There had to be *more*. If I was going to build something and create something that takes *everything* of me, to wake up each morning year after year and eat those shards of glass and stare into that abyss — and risk *failure* — there has to be more to it than a pile of ashes, more than yet another set of start-up battle scars and a scuffed reputation. Surely there has to be a pursuit of something brighter than innovation for innovation's sake? Surely there has to be something higher than the pursuit of higher profits and higher exit prices? Surely I was missing the nuance of what it means to contribute to the world — to humanity — in a *meaningful* way?

I already knew I wasn't going to be motivated enough by solely the thrill of this kind of chase again; the rules had changed. If there was no higher purpose, I wasn't playing any more. I now had enough money not to have to work. I'd sold a

At times in the silence of the night and in rare lonely moments, I come upon a sort of communion with myself and something great that is not myself.

H. G. Wells

company that I spent a third of my life building and somebody thought was special enough to buy, but it didn't feel much like I'd imagined it would. If I didn't care much about the money and 'success' from all this work in business *now*, then why on earth would I go and do it all over again if I'm just as likely not to care about the money and 'success' later? It was like a riddle that had kept hinting over the course of the decade was finally revealing itself and I was only now getting wise enough to start to piece it all together.

Pioneering for the thrill of it was just not enough; chasing a vision for the sake of a vision wasn't going to cut it; and neither was just striving to be the best in the world at whatever it was I'd chosen to strive for. The best at *what* in the world was a more important question, but perhaps being the best at something *for* the world might be the more inspiring response?

Before we'd even come through the shit, and before I even knew it myself, in my mind and my spirit, I'd stepped past the fulcrum of newly pivoting ideas of life, walking through an invisible point of no return. The most profound questions — the *biggest problems* — sprung forward and leant towards me.

What do I want to spend the days of my life building towards and contributing to?

What's the very best use of my time on this planet to live the most meaningful life I could possibly live and have the most impact I could possibly have for the benefit of the most people?

If I died tomorrow and the world asked what Derek Handley had done with his time, would I love the answer?

No. It was clear to me that I hadn't made an ounce of impact on the world at large.

At 31 though, it wasn't too late, and all was not lost. With a good 50, maybe 60, years left in me, the new question was what

Never waste a good crisis.

Niccolò Machiavelli

could I make of them all if I dedicated a life to pursuing a single purpose that was good for the world? What *could* I do with my time to die and still fall in love with the answer? What *could* I make of those years so that by their end, when visitors from Mars arrived on Earth and asked, 'What did Derek Handley *do?*' maybe, just maybe, they might be able to cite one or two things that left a dent; one or two significant things that made the world better off than it was when I arrived; one or two things that inspired others to want to do the same.

Never before had I felt so far away from an idea becoming reality. So I started where I always start — mapping these new worlds to begin a new journey. A journey in search of the real problems and opportunities — the ones, I decided, that would *define and change a generation*. My generation.

As soon as man does not take his existence for granted, but beholds it as something unfathomably mysterious, thought begins.

Albert Schweitzer

17

Change

When you start on a quest like this to find the levers that move the world, to make it a better place, to *change* it, where do you begin? While everyone around you is caught up in the day-to-day fight to survive and just push through, is it right to start asking people what the *real* problems of the world are, as if to suggest that their own problems aren't? Is it right to start asking what our moral obligations are to our fellow men, when in that time plenty of them were in a crisis of their own? I came to believe that whatever I thought were our big problems were in fact paper cuts. High-class paper cuts — problems that to others would look like luxuries.

I knew *nobody* in this new world of problem-solving; I only knew people in the world of money-making. I couldn't pick up the phone, dial a few friends and get all the answers on the state of the world, our planet, the less fortunate and the problems of society.

I began with three buckets: health, the planet, and poverty. I determined health was something I couldn't see an easy way to get involved with as I have no training; I'm not a doctor or a scientist and I imagine it's not something you can Google your way into understanding. For starters I settled on the planet and poverty as my stomping grounds and started by asking: how is poverty created and why does it persist? Why has it not been solved? If we can create the Apple Corporation, if we can create

Facebook and the internet, if we can send people to space, to the moon — *how is it possible to still have poor people?*

As a total novice I went looking for answers. I was looking to find where philanthropy or charity works and scales like business does. I was looking for anything that could convince me it would work at solving the roots of what's wrong in a way that can scale the solution to meet the size of the problem and I came across Opportunity International, a pioneer in the idea of microfinance and microfinancial services. The concept was simple: to lift people out of poverty they need access to the means that enable them to create greater incomes, often as micro-entrepreneurs, and this means access to friendly credit. Very small loans — $50, $100 — given to individuals and communities to enable them to get *ahead* in their daily trade or livelihood, to go from hand to mouth each day as a farmer or trader, to perhaps behave a little bit more like a businessperson. I took a trip with the Opportunity team to visit these people in Rwanda and Tanzania and met the living examples of the idea — the trader who, with that little extra money, can buy more stock, and at a better price, then increase the diversification of goods she could offer at any one time. She made more money, sent her children to a school that they otherwise wouldn't attend — and most importantly, could see a much brighter future for them ahead.

Does this scale? Repeat this over and over millions and millions of times across millions and millions of lives and you could imagine that it might.

I crudely sketched out how many Opportunity Internationals it would take to relieve global poverty — and wondered whether it would be possible and how long it might take? Opportunity say that each customer positively affects the lives of 10 people in their community; if they could get to 10 million customers, up from the five million they have today, that would mean a positive reach of 100 million people. If that were true, then we'd need just 20 Opportunity Internationals to scale to 10 million customers, or 50 to scale to four million, to start impacting the two billion people currently living below $2 a day. Of course it was possible. How could it not be? Difficult, but in the context of a generation? Possible.

I'm not fooling myself that these issues aren't incredibly complex and that it would be naïve and impossible to distil them into a few pages with broad-brush answers like I just have — but on the very face of it, there are more than enough resources in the world — so if business exists, poverty shouldn't.

Similarly and in parallel, I began to try to understand the difficulties facing our planet, equally if not more complex and intertwined. I started with the theory of 'peak oil' — that we are running out of fossil fuels and that there is general agreement that we need to shift the global system away from relying on it this century. Everywhere you look we've been doing it wrong — we've been fighting Mother Nature and treating her horrifically so that we can lift *our* living standards but crush hers.

These are a collection of issues and topics I had ignored for *33 years* — topics that I had relegated to the bucket to think about later — *after* I'd made my fortune and made my mark on the world. What I hadn't realised was that these were precisely the issues to try and make my mark with — not the other way around — and that they should be dealt with *as I live*, not after I've lived.

The old paradigm of fortune-hunting before philanthropy is on its way out. The old model of doing well and *then* doing good is on the decline. The new model is, do well by doing good — reinvent what it means to create companies, ventures and business models

The only place poverty belongs is in museums.

Muhammad Yunus

— ones that solve these challenges of our generation *at the same time* as creating profitable, attractive commercial outcomes. Reinvent philanthropy and social responsibility — how, where and why we give — to solve problems at their core, not the symptoms at the edge; to give as intensely as we work, not as a footnote to our living. Not after, not on the side, not as charity — but as a part and parcel of how we do business. Because business that is not good for the world, or its people, is *bad business.*

I figure we need to convince armies of the smartest people in the world to get out of the business of making a shitload of money they don't need, and get into the business of enabling millions of people to live better lives, educate their children and play a fundamental role in helping make poverty history and restoring the planet to something that resembles its former self. As simplistic and crude as my logic was and still is, it was the first time I distinctly recall working backwards from how you eliminate a plague on society in a way that scales and I'm convinced that we can do it.

Although maybe this all came later in my life than it should have, these experiences underscored to me that I was on the right path. If I believed I had talent, which I did, and energy to give, which I would, and I had the vision to see things differently, which I could — I decided that there are just too many serious challenges in the world to *not* be committed to playing the biggest part I could possibly play in resolving them.

Once we'd sold the company, people around me started to sense my increasingly shifting motivations and disposition. They could probably see the early signs the moment we'd sold that initial 19.9 per cent a year earlier. Inwardly and outwardly I was now calmer than anybody had ever known me to be. The ulcers and stomach pains were gone. I slept normally again. It was almost impossible to wind me up or stress me out, which people started to incorrectly interpret as not caring. As having lost my passion. People thought I had taken my foot off the pedal of life, that my goals weren't high enough any more and that my ambition and drive had gone. People were bemused that I appeared to be less motivated by money, by 'success', and wasn't impatiently making plans to get out there and onto another start-up to make a bigger splash, create a bigger hit and strike a bigger payday. They started to think that I was losing the plot and that I wanted to take a trip down easy street, arrogantly thinking I'd 'made it' and it was time to kick back.

There isn't anything in the world that they could have been more *wrong* about. I wanted to take them by the shoulders, shake them and whisper in their face: 'It's not me! It's you! I *have* drive. I *have* motivation. I *have* aspirations, dreams and hunger — I have it more now than ever — it's just not for the same things any longer.

'It's to become a new type of entrepreneur aimed at solving new types of problems in a new way. It's to try and help inspire a new way to think. It's to use everything I am and to put everything I have behind making the world a better place. It's to try to *change the world*. There, I said it. And if I spend the rest of my life dedicated to doing just that, then maybe — just maybe — with the help of people, friends, strangers, family — maybe, I might be able to play my part.'

The misconceptions of those who were misreading my cues were *their* problems not mine. *My* problem was that I was looking for a purpose beyond me, and I hadn't found it. I wasn't living my purpose and I had to put plans in place until I was — to step out of the charade I'd created in my *head* and lived through in my life, and to start to live through my *heart*. My problem was that I needed to spend the rest of my life living what I was now starting to believe I was *really* put here on this planet to do versus what I had tricked myself into believing I was here to do.

Each of us is here for a brief sojourn; for what purpose we know not, though we sometimes think we sense it. But even without deeper reflection, one knows from daily life that one exists for other people — first of all for those upon whose smiles and well-being our own happiness is wholly dependent, and then for the many, unknown to us, to whose destinies we are bound by the ties of sympathy . . . I must exert myself in order to give in the same measure as I have received and am still receiving.

Albert Einstein

18

Purpose

As the streets turned auburn back in New York I pulled out all my Smythson notebooks, sat to think about what lay ahead in 2012 and to review where everything stood. In the little black one, Maya and I had scribbled down a plan to gradually swap more and more of the northern winters for the southern summers until the first hundred days of every year were spent in New Zealand. We'd committed to be on the beach from January to March 2012 to be doing nothing, hitting our goal for the first time.

On that very same baby blue page, I saw that I had scrawled wistfully to the side for myself, 'A year of retreat: 2011?' with two emphatic black lines almost underscoring the question mark more than the commitment. I picked up a pen, drew a circle around the 2011 and a line out to the side where I wrote, '2012'. I had almost forgotten that I had *always* planned to do this — to take a year off and give my soul to follow my heart — and in that moment realised I was just one year behind what would probably turn out to be the single most important goal and plan I'd written on my thirtieth birthday in the Palm Springs desert. When I wrote it I didn't know what 'retreat' meant — and I didn't know in what form it would come, only that I needed it.

I pulled out the second little Smythson book — the green one outlining my core beliefs, which by this time had been written and overwritten by hand so many times that there was no room to clearly and cleanly decipher what it was I had finally decided I meant and believed in.

When we first did the deal with Meredith and after many years of searching I found myself a coach; I figure if the best sportspeople in the world should have one, then why shouldn't everybody else strive to follow suit?

Over time, Karen and I had been progressively crafting a clearer and clearer vision for my life. We got together regularly and worked closely on my next move, planning it with care. It was a steady mental grind but at least it was pushing in one direction: forward. I would occasionally have an emotional battle within myself, one that I imagine is similar to a recovering alcoholic thinking of having just one drink. As much as we made progress, during these mental bouts there was a continual undertone of the internal fight between the idea of doing well *and* doing good — and whether you can or must do one before the other.

Part of what was burning away at me was that I had in no way entered the realm of what today you might consider the world's most successful entrepreneurs — I hadn't built a billion-dollar company, I hadn't built a brand name everyone knew, I hadn't built a company that changed the way people lived all around the world. During these episodes, I felt vulnerable and that as an entrepreneur I was, in fact, quite underwhelming and still had an enormous amount to prove. I would read the TechCrunch website, which glorifies the high-growth venture start-up world beyond all respectful proportion of its place in society, and every now and then see things that would derail my day. I might see the 12-month-old iPhone app GroupMe sell for US$85 million or read about the inexplicable details of the three-year-old voucher company Groupon listing on the stock exchange for a value of more than US$10 billion. I would lose concentration on whatever I was doing at the time — my stomach would tie up in a knot. I was thinking, 'That could be me.' More than that, I was thinking, 'That *should* be me. I need to go out and do that just to underscore that *I can*.' I would then spend the next few hours thinking about all the things you could *do* with the money that would be good for the world once you'd made it. Here was the very essence of the question that kept coming back to haunt me — can't I do well and *then* do good?

'Do I need to do that *first*, Karen? Isn't that what needs to happen?'

No. Because it's a new world dawning. We are on the cusp of a new way. It's no longer a choice to do either — the only choice is *both*. I was going to stick to my still hazy vision of the future — that there is a *new* way to shape the world, that we can no longer live in a society where we create great wealth at unaccounted costs for people and the planet and in unaccountable ways and *then* turn around like heroes with our millions and billions as if none of that had ever happened, and stretch our arms out to help patch up the wounds we helped create.

That model is archaic and screwed up. It represents the Industrial Age and the twentieth-century thinking that has brought us to the very challenges we face today. If I wanted to be a player in this century, I had to play a part in driving that model back into the past, and play a part in championing a new one in its place for the future.

By this time I had switched all my reading from the Warren Buffetts and Bill Gateses on business and money to the Nelson Mandelas and Martin Luther King Jrs on meaning and mindfulness; I had renewed my passion for the Kennedys with a deep desire to learn more about Ted, and most of all Bobby, who

For too long we have tried to consume our way to prosperity. Look at the cost: polluted lands and oceans, climate change, growing scarcity of resources from food to land to fresh water, rampant inequality. We need to invent a new model; a model that offers growth and social inclusion . . . that is more respectful of the planet's finite resources. Nature has been kind to human beings, but we have not been kind to nature.

Ban Ki-moon

had now grown to become my favourite of them all. It dawned on me that these kinds of people didn't go around getting jobs or building companies — they committed and gave their lives in service to shape a better world. They challenged the normal. They pushed movements. They spoke the unspeakable. They championed new ideas and broke down old ones. And they created change for the good of all. But there was a divide between them, government and civil society and the world of commerce and entrepreneurship — as if one side makes a mess of it, and the other side cleans it up. A divide that perhaps finally breaks down with our generation? A divide falsely put up and held up by years of normality of screwing the world with your left hand and then trying to fix it with your right.

Life starts where your comfort zone ends, this much I know. I was getting into some very new territory. By this stage, I felt *sure* of what I wanted to become and the life I wanted to live. It was to live a life at the intersection of doing well for myself by doing good for others — and to inspire the next generation of dreamers and entrepreneurial leaders to follow suit.

This idea was my lighthouse, but there was still a sea of fog in my path. I decided the best way to clear it was to use up my year of retreat and just *give it away*. To donate a year of my life to a collection of whatever causes and organisations were trying to shape this *new* world; the people and experiences that would advance me to a greater understanding of the emerging wave at the intersection of profit and purpose. I would take money, jobs, start-ups and companies completely out of the equation. Of all the bets, the risks, the gambles I'd taken, this was the biggest of them all with no certain return, no sure knowledge of the rules of the game; just roll the dice, and let them land where they land.

One year. One thirty-third of what the world had so far given to me, I would put it out there and see what the universe threw back in return. I don't mean a year coming in to the local charity and doing the odd job here and there, or organising the odd fundraiser or picking up the phone every now and then to round up a few supporters for a good cause. And I don't mean a year of part-time effort a few hours a day while I fill the rest of my life with hobbies and family time and leisure and learning all those things I've *always* wanted to learn for myself like playing the piano or improving Mandarin or writing that children's book. What I mean is one year of whatever I was good at — building passionate teams, creating unique ideas, raising money off a vision, starting things from scratch, building them up a little bit, making a noise, launching a brand, making people sit up and take notice, solving problems, digital media, technology, marketing, strategic planning — *whatever it was* I could give, it was up for grabs for the organisations or people who could convince me that they could use me well and that I would add some impact and value to their dreams. What I mean is a year of *everything* I have — lived to the limit, Saturdays, Sundays, good days and bad days — *every* day just like I've lived all the other adventures I had chased around the world. What I mean is a year like I've always meant it: all or nothing.

As much as I had no idea what that would look like, I knew it would turn out just fine. I knew that by putting life as usual on hold I would learn more than any time I thought I might lose and gain far more than anything I would give.

Who to give the year to? Who exactly do you give a year of your life to? How and where exactly do you just say to somebody: do you want it?

I've learned that sometimes it's perfectly OK to hold a

Sometimes you dream the dream and sometimes the dream dreams you.

Karen Hamilton

mental image, an idea that you have a vague construct of just enough to give you shape and form but not enough to give you texture. This image I had was just the direction I wanted to head in, and to start filling in the blanks, I had three months of nothingness on the beach in New Zealand.

For someone as structured and ordered and specifically goal oriented as I am, as much as I love the *idea* of freedom within a framework, the idea that the 'dream dreams me' was one of the hardest things to come to terms with. *I* dream the dream, I demanded. *I* create my fate.

But day by day, I'm getting there.

Before we headed to New Zealand, in the first week of December 2011 I had organised for Maya and I to join the fellow Virgin Galactic future astronaut customers at the annual week-long get-together at Richard Branson's home on Necker Island in the British Virgin Islands. Before we knew it we were having the conversation on the couch that night that created yet one more transformative fork in an increasingly inspiring road.

It is, perhaps, also better, as
well as more heroical, to strike
at some daring or darling object,
and if we fail in that, to take the
consequences manfully, than
to renew the lease of a tedious,
spiritless, charmless existence,
for some worthless object.

William Hazlitt

19

Necker

It's not every day somebody you don't know very well at all walks up to you and says, 'Here, would you like a year of my life?' but that's pretty much what happened. As we got stuck into the conversation Richard got practical.

'How much money did you make from your business?' he asked.

'Enough to be able to do this,' I skirted.

He drilled down — and asked me a figure — did I have that figure in the bank, a figure that I think he assumed was of some significance in this context. He was trying to draw me out to be sure I could afford what I'd offered. I lied and said, 'Yes, about that.' He asked me if I had a mortgage, had we paid off our house? I lied again and said, 'Yes, we have.' He asked me how old I was and if I had any children — that was easier — I told the truth and said, 'Thirty-three and no, not yet — but we want some. Soon.'

By 33, Richard Branson was a world-famous billionaire who had sold Virgin Records and started a global airline — I'm not sure what he made of my answer. Had I done enough? Was I accomplished enough at the age I was? Was I competent enough to work on his projects to change the world? Was he putting himself in my shoes at that age and thinking about what he was thinking about back then? Was he thinking about his own kids, who were roughly my age and whether we'd get along? I have no idea. I don't know why it was an important question but he asked it as if it was.

He paused, and moved on; and looked at me. 'You have to take care of your family. As long as you can take care of your family.'

And I was confident I could. I had put things in place, I wasn't about to plunge us into struggle again — the truth is, we live modestly and we had means enough. I never would have committed to this notion if I wasn't 100 per cent convinced we would be perfectly fine. To get some ideas flowing, I said:

'So these are some of the things I can do — I can start things, I can pick up from a blank piece of paper and turn ideas into reality — I can start companies, create brands, I know about technology, I have a good grasp on where it's going. I can build teams. I understand marketing.'

He began to share some of the various things he and Jean, who heads up Virgin Unite — his foundation — were doing.

'We are working with Wild Aid — tackling the endangered species lists to bring awareness and action to certain situations. For example, the sharks, the sharks are being decimated — and the practice of finning to make the soup — the shark's fin soup in China and Hong Kong. It's terrible — so we are working on that. Last month with Yao Ming in China we were working on that.'

Richard speaks slowly. He pauses sometimes and even stutters as he gathers the words he wants. Sometimes he just stops, thinks and concludes, 'Yeah, umm, yeah,' without adding anything new, ending the line of thought.

'I've heard of that,' I said. 'I think it's really great — but it's not so much where my passion lies — I do appreciate it, I appreciate the scale of the problem but it's just not what is calling me — yet. So I wouldn't probably want to get into that so much. I am on this track about the idea of using business as a force for good — somewhere in there I can get really passionate.'

'Right. Good. Well that's good — you've got to follow your heart and do what you love. OK, so no Wild Aid. Well, we have the Carbon War Room — do you know much about that?'

I admitted I knew very little. He went on to explain that the Carbon War Room had been set up to tackle large-scale business opportunities that if unlocked and implemented will create gigatons of carbon emission reductions — a gigaton is one billion tons. In other words, trying to use business as a means to uncover opportunities that make money, while significantly reducing global warming.

'I'm interested in that — I've been really interested in electric cars recently — sounds very interesting, we could perhaps see where I could help, but I assume you've got a team up and running already?'

'Well, we have this other idea — we have been thinking . . . To create a group of global business leaders — to stand up for a new way of doing business. To champion the idea that business needs to change itself, and fundamentally rethink its role in society to help make the world a better place. To try and change a few rules. We've been thinking about this idea for some time but I don't think we've managed to find anyone to help make it happen.'

He expanded and told me about the concept that was vaguely inspired by The Elders group that he and musician Peter Gabriel had created four years earlier with Nelson Mandela and Archbishop Desmond Tutu. The Elders were formed as an independent group of public figures and global statesmen to act as a collective to use their wisdom for the benefit of humanity. What had sprung from it a couple of years later was the notion that the world needed an equivalent for business — especially in the wake of the recent financial crisis and profound lack of visible moral leadership in industry. The idea, as it stood then, was simply to create a new global leadership collective, business leaders standing together to act and fight for a new way of doing business. For doing business by doing good for the planet and its people in order to ultimately do well for their shareholders.

There was nothing in the world that sounded more like what I needed to be doing in my life.

It was so conceptual — and very hard to know exactly what I was getting myself into — but there was no way that there was a bigger idea in the world that was more aligned with the path that I wanted to be on than this one.

Before the wine was finished, we had agreed to join forces and that I would help spearhead the nameless initiative — to help create this organisation to start and build something that will do its part to shape a kinder face to capitalism at a time when the world so desperately needs it.

20

Africa

'Did you get my email?' he asked, sitting in his washed-out board shorts gathered among a few of the Virgin Galactic staff around the cushions in the corner of Turtle Beach the next morning.

'No . . . when did you send it?' I replied, as I crunched up the sand from the water's edge.

We had just parked our little Hobie Cat sailboat next to the rest of the fleet after coming near last in the race around the island.

'Earlier . . . a couple of hours ago maybe?' he replied.

It was about 11 on a predictably flawless day in the British Virgin Islands. I'd missed it.

'Well, I think I was busy heading down to start losing this race probably, just as the email arrived — what did it say?'

'I am heading out later today. Do you want to come along. To Africa?'

I couldn't quite compute what we were talking about. I was on Necker Island — I was already *in* paradise. It had tennis courts and turtles, beaches and blue sea, flamingos and morning stars that rose from the darkness and more than the senses of reality could bear. We weren't even set to leave yet for another couple of days.

'Jean will be there. You can meet her and spend time together. And we will be visiting some of the work in the field that we support and our safari game reserve so you can see what we do,' he continued.

I quickly tried to connect the dots, but like a flooded engine, my brain just refused to start. Turn the crank. Nothing. Turn the crank. Nothing.

It just hung. Suspended. On repeat in my head was, 'But I have a meeting with Kraft on Monday in Chicago.' I needed a reboot and a time-out. It must have taken me about five or 10 seconds — which is an awkwardly long time in the middle of a conversation.

'Hang on — go to Africa — where are you going? When do you leave? For how long?'

I asked about three or four very stupid questions. Practical. But stupid. Like any of these things mattered. How could they matter?

'My plane is leaving at about three, so we'd have to get out of here and be at Red Dock at about two — spending the day in London then to Kenya, and then South Africa — and we'd need to get you tickets from London and some other bits and pieces — we can take care of that easily enough. But we'd need to know quickly.'

'And Maya?' I tested.

'Of course — in fact, you only get to come if she comes!'

'Right.'

The brain was still catching up with the conversation. I was just looking at the Galactic team perched next to him, Dave and Stephen, and they were just looking right back at me as if to say, 'Well?' They must see this kind of thing all the time, I thought. I felt like someone was playing a fantastical practical joke on me — but I'd read that Richard Branson made decisions like this. I knew that it was real.

'Right. If you could just give me a minute. Let me go and

talk with her . . . let's see what she says.'

Maya was over by the drinks and fruit set up under the trees. The Kraft meeting was looping in my mind — and for about a minute as I walked over to her, I was actually considering the options and thinking about the dates and logistics — as if to consider that there *were* any other options other than yes? Of course there weren't.

I walked towards Maya, up the sand, and waved her over coolly as if to talk about the weather. In hushed tones that weren't hiding to anyone watching that there was something seriously interesting being talked about, I began.

'So Richard just asked if we want to tag along on his plane and head to Africa with him for a week. Kenya, South Africa, the game reserves. We'd have to spend a day in London on the way first though . . .'

I was now looking into a set of disbelieving and confused eyes, flipping between sceptical squints and widened incredulity, just like mine must have looked only seconds earlier.

'What? When?'

'Now. We have to go *now* if we want to go. No lunch, no fruit — we have to go pack and get our passport details and all that.'

'No,' she said. 'No, I don't think that's a good idea — no. I think you say, no, thank you that's very kind but no, we can't accept that . . . but thank you very much.'

Out of politeness she defaulted to how you might react when somebody offers you a lift home that would detour well out of their way to drop you off.

'No. Come on. We're going. Don't be ridiculous. Africa is on our list of places to see together. Game reserves on our list of things to do together. We're being invited. Let's go. Last night I gave a year of my life away to him. This morning he takes us to Africa — this is the way the universe works, this is how good things happen — there's a reason for everything. This is the next step on this journey. We have to go.'

We conferred for about 60 seconds and we both realised there was only one answer.

'Yes, Richard — we'd like to. We're very excited — thank you very much for the offer. We're really looking forward to meeting Jean and visiting Africa. We'll go back to our rooms and pack up — what next?'

Like a genie, Richard's smiling assistant Sam and her ever-helpful voice appeared over the phone and a series of emails arrived to help us through everything. Before anything could sink in, we'd called my sister-in-law in London to arrange to meet her for lunch, everything was set and we'd pushed off from the Necker Red Dock, skipped our way to Tortola Airport, stepped up off the tarmac and had settled into our seats aboard *Galactic Girl*.

As the jet's engines powered us toward the skies, I could feel the weight of my life shifting heavily in a new direction. What lay ahead? Who knew. Other than that, it would look absolutely nothing like what we were leaving behind.

It's only when we truly know and understand that we have a limited time on earth — and that we have no way of knowing when our time is up — that we might begin to live each day to the fullest, as if it was the only one we had.

Elisabeth Kübler-Ross

Starting

A few months later, alongside Richard, Jean and their friend Jochen Zeitz, I kicked off as the founding CEO of what we've ended up calling The B Team. We began the search to create a collective of the most inspiring leaders from around the world to help chart a new course for business — a Plan B, for a better future. A future where business becomes a driving force for social, environmental and economic benefit — and understands its responsibility this century to not only solve the problems it has largely helped to create or has ignored, but to do so profitably, in new ways with all the good that business and entrepreneurship have to bring. A future too, where whatever I do, however I live and all that I give needs to align with this new world, embodying its spirit — and I'm only just starting to figure out how.

As much as I know I'll look back in 10 years and know that I didn't understand things at all — today it's enough to say that I think I understand things pretty well, for now. After all the acts I got wrong and all the mistakes I've made, I'm not entirely sure that I didn't 'get it' all throughout or whether it was more that I wasn't really listening to what the universe was trying to tell me. As much by designing the things I wanted to happen, forced things I never thought about to happen to me — and as much as the fate I tried to bend, ultimately bent me — this time I think I've got it right.

If you *don't* think you've got it right — if you have the feeling that you know what you're doing is not what you were meant to be doing with your time on this planet — you have a bit of work to do, but take comfort in knowing that by just knowing this, you've at least started. To ask: Whose life are you living? Whose purpose are you fulfilling? What are your reasons for being here? Who we are and what we think of ourselves changes constantly — a symbol of the ongoing pilgrimage of awakening that we are all on.

Have faith. If you keep looking and pushing, you'll get there. 'Some day' may never come, but today is always here. There is only one now — and this moment is your life. If you wait for 'until' to search for your calling, you may die before it arrives. There is always another level you could chase before you're 'ready', always more money, always a better job, always a better home.

You're ready now.
You were ready yesterday.
Never grow up.
Never give up.
Begin.
Become.

When you feel electrified and aligned. When you see things you never used to see. When you pray to do more for others than for yourself. When you wish for the world to be better through the things that you achieve. You will know that you have left the walking dead and have joined the walking living.

But what do I know? Of all the things I could or should have learned, there's one thing I suspect I now understand — that I'm starting a new journey. All over again. Once more. The beginning of yet another beginning. And the *one* thing I know for sure? After all these years living from start to (eventually) get to my heart — from now on, I'm only living from heart to start.

Wonderful things will never be done if you do not do them.

Richard Branson

THE PROUST
QUESTIONS

1. What is your idea of perfect happiness?

Living in tune with the universe! Spending all the right time and energy on all the right places and people. Perfectly balancing one eye on the long and one eye on the short...

2. What is your greatest fear?

Of not having made a meaningful difference.

3. What is the trait you most deplore in yourself?

Visible impatience

4. What is the trait you most deplore in others?

I can't quite decide between lack of integrity to follow through; weak desire to constantly seek to be better; or those who believe they have no duty to do what they can to make the world a better place...

5. Which living person do you most admire?

I don't think one single person stands out from the rest... of those who are dead — Bobby Kennedy & William Wilberforce.

6. What is your greatest extravagance?

I eat what I want. A ticket to space.

7. What is your current state of mind?

Calm. Optimistic. Grateful.

8. What do you consider the most overrated virtue?

Being reasonable. Is that a virtue?

9. On what occasion do you lie?

To convince myself I'm capable.

10. What do you most dislike about your appearance?

I could always be a little taller.

11. Which living person do you most despise?

—

12. What is the quality you most like in a man?

Open vulnerability — and purposeful spirit

13. What is the quality you most like in a woman?

Grace — and purposeful spirit

14. Which words or phrases do you most overuse?

—

15. What or who is the greatest love of your life?

*What? : Challenge & Vision. The things people say
can't be done.*
Who ? : Maya.

16. When and where were you happiest?

Now and here.

17. Which talent would you most like to have?

Natural musical genius. Photographic memory.

18. If you could change one thing about yourself, what would
it be?

To become consistently mindful and present in the moment.

19. What do you consider your greatest achievement?

*To have begun to discover the life I'm meant
to live*

20. If you were to die and come back as a person or a thing, what would it be?

Myself — in a thousand years. Failing that — a comet.

21. Where would you most like to live?

With one foot in the centre of the world and one foot on the edge — between New York & New Zealand.

22. What is your most treasured possession?

My mind. If I lost it, I think I'll be sad.

23. What do you regard as the lowest depth of misery?

The inability to think for one's self.

24. What is your favorite occupation?

To shape visions & turn them into reality. Failing that — a better writer and a philosopher.

25. What is your most marked characteristic?

Determination. Fearlessness.

26. What do you most value in your friends?

Loyalty. Being constructively challenged.

27. Who are your favourite writers?

Emerson. Michael Lewis.

28. Who is your hero of fiction?

Howard Roark — not because of _what_ he believed,
but because of how independently & ferociously he
believed it til the end.

29. Which historical figure do you most identify with?

—

30. Who are your heroes in real life?

They are mostly dead. Picasso. Benjamin Franklin.
Elon Musk. Alexander the Great ... Gandhi.
The Medici.

31. What are your favourite names?

Finn. Emerson. Maya. Cleo. Kennedy.

32. What is it that you most dislike?

Solving symptoms; not causes.
Weak questions.
Excuses.

33. What is your greatest regret?

Not saying goodbye to my grandmother, Poh Poh.

34. How would you like to die?

With my mind in tact. Peacefully and in my own time, surranded by family and friends of all ages. Having been intimately involved in the planning of the ~~the~~ celebrations to follow.

35. What is your motto?

I still don't have one good enough to share.

Long afterwards, she was to remember that moment when her life changed its direction. It was not predestined; she had a choice. Or it seemed that she had. To accept or refuse. To take one turning down the crossroads to the future or another.

Evelyn Anthony

Thank You

Mum and Dad; Geoffrey and Anna; Calum; Keiji and Francesca; Aunty Zarina and Uncle Frank; Aunty Fiz and Uncle Jay; Peter, Greta and Molly; Dan and Shareen; Jenny and John; Jane Macky; Jo Kelly; Charlotte Glennie; Millie and Les; Kevin Roberts; Steven and Jane; Ken Kwok; Sir Ray Avery; Sir Richard Branson; Jean Oelwang; Jochen and Andrea; John Elkington; Heerad Sabeti; Karen Hamilton; Alyson Shontell; Srini and Brani; Jagan, Jagadish, Satya Naveen and Pardha; Darnell, Ghanum, Mitch and James; Howard Hunt; Jeff Arbour; Grant Baker and Geoff Ross; Nihal Mehta; Nicole Amodeo; Mark D'arcy; Karen Uribe; Wendy Riches and John Zieser; Jessica Kolski; Jennifer Mitrenga; Jim O'Mahony; Rebecca Mills; Andrew Hamilton; Alistair Helm; Roz Turner; Geoff Bramley; Murray Bevan; Tom Eslinger; Brooke Howard Smith; Andre de Frere; Kyle and Tim; Shelley Campbell; Erica Crawford; Sam Johnson; Andrew Jacobs; Karen and Mikhail; Keith Norris; Emma Peckham; Antonia Prebble; Kimberley Crossman; Lee Prebble; Shae Stirling; Kerry Spackman; Shelley, Martin and Bea; Peter Morrison; John Hart, Jock Irvine and Richard Waddel; Paul Philips, Grant Stembridge, Rob Butler, Ross Wales and Chu Ki; Hubert Tose; Tim Wilson; Jamie McClellan; Elon Musk; Jen Mitrenga.

And so we strive, tirelessly on.